Praise for

YOU HEAL YOU

INSPIRATIONAL AND MIRACULOUS HEALING STORIES OF MODERN DAY WARRIORS (2016)

WINNER OF THE 2017 INTERNATIONAL EXCELLENCE BODY, MIND, SPIRIT BOOK AWARD IN THE HEALING CATEGORY

"... like the kind, encouraging words of a dear friend..."
—Tamara Benson, Manhattan Book Review

"... a thoughtful book about taking responsibility for one's...life and...health. *You Heal You* imparts hope that, despite obstacles, life can change for the better..."
—Catherine Thureson, Clarion Review

"Readers [will] come away feeling better."
—Blue Ink Review

"... Each page carries a message, a laugh, a tear, and inspiration for readers to look at their life and question whether they are listening to their own team of angels..."
—Amy Synoracki, San Francisco Book Review

You Heal You

THRIVING AFTER ILLNESS, PAIN, AND LOSS

INSPIRATIONAL & MIRACULOUS HEALING STORIES OF 18 MODERN DAY WARRIORS

JANE G. DOYLE

UPDATED 2022 EDITION

First edition published 2016.

ISBN-9798836650674

Printed by Kindle Direct Publishing
Printed in the United States of America

Cover design by Jeff Hall
Cover illustration by Troth Adan, istock.com
Back Cover photography by Paul Dabrowski
Graphic design by Jeff Hall Design, jh.design@rcn.com

A version of Jane Borden's "The Messenger Bag of Happiness" was previously published as "Still Life: How I Learned to Flush a Toilet with My Feet" in *O'Henry Magazine* (November 2012). Reprinted with permission from the author.

"A Lourdes Christmas Miracle: Delizia Cirolli-Costa" was originally published as "Delizia Cirolli-Costa," in *Cures of Lourdes Recognized as Miraculous by the Church*, Bureau des Constatations Médicales, Sanctuaire Notre-Dame de Lourdes (May 2011). All rights reserved. Reprinted with permission from the Medical Bureau of Lourdes.

The poem in chapter 29 (Doss, Can you Imagine?) was originally published in *Poésies Naïves et Spontanées* by Charles Leuret. Reprinted with permission from the author.

Disclaimer and Terms of Use: Effort has been made to ensure that the information in the book is accurate and complete; however, the author and publisher do not warrant the accuracy of the information. The author and publisher do not hold any responsibility for errors, omissions, or contrary interpretation of the subject matter herein. This book is for motivational and informational purposes only. It is not to be considered rendering medical advice or services. If you feel you have a health problem, consult your physician or health practitioner.

YouHealYou™ titles may be purchased in bulk for educational, business, fundraising, and sales promotion use. Contact jane@youinspireyou.net.

To Heavenly Team Jane

Contents

Introduction

You heal you," my inner voice whispered. I was a fifty-four-year-old investment advisor from Chicago, and I hadn't felt well in decades. Spring 2009, I was in the countryside in Abadiânia, Brazil, visiting the renowned healing center Casa de Dom Inacio de Loyola. I had just heard the widely held, local belief that our actions often contribute to our illnesses. And if God heals us without us doing our part, then the symptoms will likely return. This aha moment changed my life.

I was inspired to take back control of my health. I became the chairman of my wellness board, head coach of my life, and chief scientist of my personal healing solution. Simply put, Jane needed to be accountable for Jane. I was motivated to become responsible for my actions and redirect my thinking to new ideas and ways to get well. It made sense. If I was contributing to my illnesses through my actions, then I could contribute to my healing by changing my behavior. After thirty years of struggling to find answers to my declining health, I began to heal.

I had assumed all along that I was doing my part by spending time and money going from doctor to doctor looking for a solution. But I was just following orders. By giving up control to the process, I paid a heavy toll: I got sicker. I had fallen from a state of rarely being sick to one of seldom feeling well—with no known cure.

It all started in the early 1980s, several years before I moved to Chicago. I was in my mid-twenties and began to get headaches. All day. Every day. It was as if someone turned on a light switch and forgot to turn it off.

At first, the headaches were only mildly distracting. By the time I arrived in the Midwest, I was a frequent visitor to many doctors and even tried a pain management clinic. I willingly became a pincushion for pain medications and a trial participant for new drugs. Nothing worked.

As the years passed, my symptoms bloomed like a magnolia in a greenhouse. To each of my afflictions, doctor after doctor agreed, "I have no idea why you are experiencing these symptoms." From the initial headaches to chronic fatigue syndrome (CFS); to massive and rapid weight gain; to chest pains, constant neck pain, and continual flu-like symptoms; to ringing in my ears and still more symptoms, I was told:

"Cause unknown."

"I don't know why."

"I can't help you."

Reviewing my organized, detailed, and thick notebook of medical tests and reports, a doctor said, "Many people like you, Jane, often don't make it." I did not have to ask him what he meant. I knew. It was tough going. I felt like Humpty Dumpty after his great fall. All the great doctors couldn't put me together again.

My three decades of pain were earth-shattering and changed me as a person. I was stripped of the insignificant and left with the core of who I am—not what others wanted me to be. Pain has a way of burning away the trivial.

Luckily for me (and thanks to my mother's can-do personality and my father's bloodline), my inner Scottish warrior emerged fueling me with the determination to survive (not lose) this battle and keep looking up (not down). I took it one day at a time—even ten seconds at a time when necessary.

I used my limited energy to stay focused on what I did want in my life. I wanted to have close relationships again. I wanted to go out with my friends. I wanted to stay up past 6:00 p.m. and not collapse into bed from pain and fatigue. I wanted to date again. To stop spending money on medical bills. To be well. To enjoy my passions. To enjoy life. To belly laugh. To be glad to be alive. I was done with pain—physical, emotional, and spiritual. I was prepared to give my all just to be normal again.

I did give it my all, and slowly I recovered. And you know what? As challenging, painful, and lonely as those years were, I would welcome the same experience just to get to where I am today. Prayer to God: please, though, give me several lifetimes of R & R first.

***

You Heal You: Inspirational & Miraculous Healing Stories of Modern Day Warriors retraces my healing journey and those of others just like me and perhaps like you. Their stories motivated me to keep going until I found my personal wellness prescription. I hope they will do the same for you.

My goal in sharing our sometimes difficult experiences is to inspire, redirect, and heal. To inspire the belief that anything is possible. To redirect our thoughts and actions to find a healing solution (and not limit yourself like I did by continuing prescribed treatments that didn't work). And even if our symptoms are the same, to encourage us to create a healing formula based on our unique needs and circumstances. To inspire us to take responsibility for our health and actions so we can heal ourselves. To evolve into modern day warriors and rescue ourselves. My ultimate wish is for you to have a life full of joy.

You Heal You is arranged in four parts, according to my three stages of recovery and then, the healing stories by others. I describe the fourteen steps I took on my stairway to joy, what I call "my life's journey." These steps were also used in varying combinations by the other storytellers in the fourth and final part.

Part I: Jane the Apprentice (2002–2008). In Scotland, in 2002, I sat at the feet of my ancestral elders. Grounded in my love for this Celtic country, I learned to listen to my highest wisdom—my inner voice—and became strong enough to set out to find my remedies.

Part II: Jane the Explorer (2009–2012). In Brazil, in 2009, I witnessed healing miracles in others and came to expect my own. I traveled the world seeking healing cures to create my own unique healing formula.

Part III: Jane the Inspirer (2013–). Home in America, since 2013, I became an apprentice once again to learn how to sing my joy and encourage others to do the same.

Part IV: Stories of Other Modern Day Warriors. Seventeen storytellers share their self-healing experiences. They built a stairway to joy using my steps in some variation. They skipped, returned to, paused on, and even added steps in their own unique way.

My healing journey was prompted by love—love triggered by an act of destruction. The terrorist attacks of 9/11 (September 11, 2001) crystallized for me that life is short. I was motivated to recapture joy in my life and to tackle one item on my bucket list: go to Scotland. I was passionate about this Celtic country that I had visited only in my imagination.

Five months later, around Valentine's Day, I was on a plane to Edinburgh. As Jane the Apprentice, I began to find—even if unwittingly—the tools I needed to heal myself. Some of my symptoms eased in Scotland. Had the physical land energized me? Had the joy I felt there distracted me? Could I recreate these positive results back home? I concluded love and passion are the greatest remedies.

I made seven visits to Scotland in six years, and learned the first six tools I would use for my recovery. Following my gut. Being in the moment. Leaving my comfort zones. Seeing the good in everything. Listening to my body. Pausing, but never giving up. I grew stronger and was soon able to maintain my Scottish glow between visits and at home in Chicago.

After my seventh trip to Scotland, while pausing on a stairway landing, I heard about the Scottish physician David Mickel who was using an innovative program to successfully treat patients with CFS. What are the odds I'd hear about a doctor from my beloved Scotland curing in others one of my most devastating symptoms? It prompted me to leave a comfort zone so I could work with Dr. Mickel and proved to be a major turning point for me. I have come to call these what-are-the-odds coincidences "angel tracks," signs that my angels are around to help and nudge me along.

I had always been dedicated to my recovery, but after being inspired by my successes with Dr. Mickel, I became determined to consider not only traditional but also non-traditional treatments. This triggered my next growth stage, as Jane the Explorer. I actively sought remedies and healing partners—wherever it may lead. And I had a ball.

In 2009, I traveled to the Casa in Brazil healing center and had the aha moment to be accountable for myself. Gripping the reins of my recovery, I took five more steps on my stairway to joy. Expecting my miracles. Taking responsibility for my life. Investing in myself. Finding appropriate healing partners. And creating my personal program for wellness, what I call a "unique healing formula." In *You Heal You*, our storytellers created their unique healing formula using steps that overlap in part. Yours may, too.

I continued to actively seek out those who could support my healing, but now I added God's squad. I had been relying on the wrong kings and king's men (just like Humpty Dumpty had). It is God—that great universal force of love—who can do anything. The only limitation God has is what I place on God. I have always believed in prayer, but after realizing in Brazil, the power of unseen help available to me, I renewed my efforts with intent. The unseen help was Heavenly Team Jane (that is, God and God's squad including Christ, my guardian angels, and any other divine beings of light). Since humans had had no answers for me, I invited Heavenly Team Jane to assist my miraculous recovery.

Desperation may have led me to the Casa, but hope followed me home. I became a card-carrying believer in miracles, convinced that miracles exist and can happen to anyone. I witnessed healing miracles that I had been told were not possible. I had been told for three decades that there were no solutions for my ailments and no hope. For me to move forward, I needed to believe the impossible could become possible—my definition of "miracle." I needed to believe miracles could happen to me. I needed to believe I could be healed and get my life back. But first, I had to fall off my wall of beliefs. My prized new belief is, as philosopher Epictetus said, "It's not what happens to you, but how you react that matters."

Soon after I returned to Chicago, I kept hearing the following parable. In paraphrase,

When a fierce storm was predicted to flood a town, the people of the community were advised to evacuate immediately. One of its citizens was a person of great faith and decided when he heard the warning to have faith that God would send a miracle to save him. One of his neighbors offered to drive him to safety, but he declined saying that he had faith God would save him. When the water rose to his porch, a man in a canoe paddled by and offered him a seat in his canoe. Again, he declined saying he had faith that God would save him. As the floodwaters rose to his second floor, a policeman in a boat came and offered to take him to safety, but again he refused saying he had faith that God would save him. Finally, after he climbed onto his roof, a rescue helicopter pilot came by with a lowered rope ladder. Again he refused help. Eventually the man drowned. In Heaven, he asked God why God didn't answer his prayers and save him. God said that his prayers were answered. He had been sent a warning, a car, a canoe, a boat, and a helicopter.

I got it. Maybe my prayers were being answered all along, but I had let them pass me by just like the faithful man in the story. Now I had to be on alert and open to heavenly helpful hints. What are the odds that I would keep hearing this story soon after returning from Brazil?

In America, from 2013, I was well enough to begin a second apprenticeship—this time, as Jane the Inspirer—and take the last three of fourteen steps on my stairway to joy. I am learning to: live me healing me, sing my joy, and become a happy healed healer.

Along the way, I continued to uncover other modern day warriors' healing stories and their treatment methods. I share my joy by inspiring others in local storytelling events and educational seminars, via the website youinspireyou.net, and now in book form with the publication of *You Heal You.*

I am an ordinary person who has experienced something extraordinary. I firmly believe you don't have to be special to experience a miracle and heal yourself. We all have the innate capacity to contribute to our recovery, become modern day warriors, and rescue ourselves. Be inspired to use our stories as models for your own vision and healing journey. Take the stairs with Jane. Let life changing stories change your life.

PART I.

Jane the Apprentice

(2002–2008)

I have a great affection for all things Scottish, especially the Highlands. I love the brogue accent. I love the mystical legends. I love the lochs (lakes), the openness and friendliness of the people, and the fiddles and bagpipes. Ever heard "Amazing Grace" on the bagpipes? Oh, I love the misty, windy weather. I love the actual land. I love its medieval history, and even own a medieval Scottish coin. My favorite books are the historical novels by Nigel Tranter. And did I mention I really, really love a man in a kilt?

My love affair started in 1995 with the Mel Gibson movie *Braveheart*. Something awoke inside me as I watched the epic medieval battle to liberate Scotland from the rule of Edward I of England. The film may have roused my sleeping passion, but it was a catastrophe that prompted me to go there in reality instead of in my fantasies. The 9/11 (September 11, 2001) terrorist attacks on American soil inspired me to fulfill a dream on my bucket list. I would go to the Scottish Highlands.

I had a strong, unshakable urge that I needed to travel alone. When I made plans to go back with anyone else, my arrangements were upended and I'd have to go alone. This continued to happen, which hardly seemed coincidental. I have come to call these "angel tracks," evidence that my guardian angels are present and nudging me in the right direction. My guardian angels are part of my Heavenly Team Jane, along with God and God's squad (Christ, angels, and other divine beings of light). I suspect that Heavenly Team Jane wanted me to travel solo so I could learn to rely more on my inner voice. With no distractions, I could hear this voice of wisdom more easily. I came to love the freedom of just being me and discovered I really like myself and enjoy my company—especially my sense of humor.

And so February 2002, I was on the plane to Edinburgh. I chose to travel around Valentine's Day because I considered the trip as a valentine to my soul. I arrived in the ancient land of lochs and mystical legends expecting a romantic vacation and to find what had been tugging at my soul. Heavenly Team Jane had another agenda: hard work and personal growth. I was Mel Gibson's understudy. I was cast as Braveheart. I visited Scotland seven times usually around Valentine's Day over six years. Each time, I was cast as a warrior learning skills to rescue myself.

One of the first skills I learned was to never give up. Driving on the left side of the road was terrifying. I was discouraged, convinced my mystical Scotland was a pipe dream. After my first two days, I was on the verge of admitting this soul adventure was a total bust. Why would I ever take my first vacation alone over Valentine's to a country that rains, rains, rains, and where people drive on the wrong side of the road? I hit bottom the night of the lover's holiday sitting in my room at an Inverness bed-and-breakfast. I decided, "I am out of here." I woke to a sunny day and so, felt a wee better. I decided to give it one more day. Staying the course for just a little longer was life changing and prompted my first Celtic mystery.

While continuing my trek north, I stopped at a Glenmorangie whiskey distillery near the medieval town of Tain. I got out of my car, and a miracle happened. I was hit full force with the mystical sensation that my soul had been yearning for. I can't tell you what the sensation was or what triggered it, but it stayed with me the rest of the trip. I am so grateful I didn't turn around and go home. If I had, I would have missed an opportunity to become Jane the Apprentice.

During this period, I learned six vital skills from Heavenly Team Jane, which I describe in the following chapters and highlight below.

Following My Gut. In 1993 (nine years before my Scottish trips) while preparing for surgery, I received a glimpse of a valuable ally. (Chapter 1, On the Gurney)

Being in the Moment. Later, driving in Scotland, I had to stay present not to run over schoolchildren at the crosswalk. (Chapter 2, Out of My Head)

Leaving My Comfort Zones. I was forced to face an aspect of myself that I wanted to hide. I was afraid to let the black cat out of the bag. I had an affinity for the woo woo. (Chapter 3, The Blob)

Seeing the Good. I had a mystical experience on another trip to Scotland, and my reaction was negative. My strong initial aversion masked the golden key to my healing. (Chapter 4, Good Dragons)

Listening to My Body. Ancient Celtic rocks gave me useful feedback about my body. (Chapter 5, A Rock-Solid Relationship)

Pausing, but Never Giving Up. After completing an obstacle course of my worst nightmares, I witnessed a miracle on the craggy shore of Scotland. (Chapter 6, A Fair-Weathered Angel)

In addition to my six experiences, I mention other storytellers who used the same tools to self-heal. Their accounts, which appear in Part IV, support my belief that these tools are accessible to all of us. You just have to open the wee valentine to your big, brave soul.

1

Following My Gut

On the Gurney

"Pull it, Jane. Just pull it." As I lay on the hospital gurney, the insistent voice was urging me to extract a tooth that by every logical evaluation was perfectly fine. I was listening to my gut instead of to the conventional wisdom of my competent doctors. My inner physician's advice was right on and set the foundation for a turning point in my healing journey.

It was 1993, and I had been suffering with daily headaches for over ten years. All day, every day, and getting worse. I was on a regular regimen of antibiotics to combat recurring sinus infections. Nothing helped. I was at the hospital that day for my third sinus operation. I asked my doctor to pull a specific tooth during surgery because I could not shake the feeling that the tooth had something to do with my chronic headaches and sinus problems. He assured me that the tests showed nothing warranting the extraction but agreed to my request.

As I waited to go into surgery, another doctor came by to confirm I wanted to go ahead with what was in his view "an unnecessary procedure." That's right. Two esteemed doctors from one of the best hospitals in the country questioned my decision. But I was spot on. After the tooth was pulled, we found a new, clean pocket in my sinus. The root of an infected tooth that had previously been removed had been feeding bacteria into my sinus cavity, something that did not show up on x-rays or scans. I have not had another sinus surgery or chronic sinusitis since, and it has been over twenty years.

Then, I wondered briefly if my gut knows best, but I dismissed it. Eight years later, when I began training as Jane the Apprentice,

Heavenly Team Jane directed me back to this thought. Thus, I am impressed by how quickly Lucette Doss, a *You Heal You* modern day warrior, acted on a nudge. (Chapter 29, Can You Imagine?)

Intuition is now my life's compass pointing me in the right direction. People refer to this as listening to your gut, having a hunch, a deep knowing, your instinct, and the little voice inside your head. I call it "Heavenly Team Jane." When I hear myself say, "What are the odds?" that something happened, it is a pretty good indication my advisory team of divine beings is present.

I am recognizing Heavenly Team Jane's guidance. It is consistently positive and never negative. The messages are not judgmental or qualified with a "but." The gentle taskmasters honor my decisions and wait patiently. Many times, the advice makes no sense, but proves to be infallible. When I trust and accept my inner wisdom, I find out there was a good reason for the nudges. When I don't heed the advice, I get to the same place but the route is usually longer and more difficult. I hear my intuition most clearly during quiet times, such as in prayer, meditation, the shower, and yoga class.

My inner wisdom was always there. I used to hear it faintly, but my analytical mind often overrode it. February 2002, I took the bold step of following it by going to Scotland alone. For ten days, I put my instinct in the driver's seat. I was a bit unnerved and definitely outside my comfort zone, but I got the hang of it.

A year later back in Scotland, I shook up my plans and suddenly changed my itinerary just because I got the urge to go left instead of right. An old voice said, "Jane, you're crazy. Here by dragons! [a medieval phrase for 'danger'] You don't even know what's to the left." God forbid, I had not analyzed the risks. Yes, I turned left. And I had an amazing healing adventure. I cried cleansing tears in a small Highlands village church in Fortingall, where, according to legend, Christ visited. Then, in Killin, with my fingers crossed, I held the healing rocks of Saint Fillan. My day ended on the sacred island of Iona, and

I had telling dreams. By simply changing directions, left rather than right, I discovered the rewards of following my gut. I had come a long way in one short year.

Trust in my intuition strengthened with each subsequent trip to Scotland. I tested it from time to time until I had a proven track record. Today, I listen closely to my inner whispers and when I get one of my firm knowings, I follow it—even if it's contrary to the advice of well-meaning people. When Heavenly Team Jane, my reliable ally, speaks, I listen.

2

Being in the Moment
Out of My Head

Before I became Jane the Apprentice in Scotland, I thought of myself as the Analyzer. I was not very aware of my surroundings, since I spent most of my time in my head. I was great at problem solving, evaluating financial balance sheets, and projecting scenarios (usually worst-case ones) for myself. I spent a lot of time strategizing the next steps on my to-do list and re-running past programs in my mind. Often I would get home from work unable to remember having driven there. I was disconnected and not living in the now. Life was passing me by. This all changed when I arrived in Scotland in 2002. I was forced to stay alert.

With two suitcases, bed-and-breakfast vouchers, and my car rental agreement, I arrived midday at the Edinburgh airport. My destination was St. Andrews, about eighty-four kilometers, just over fifty miles, away. After getting into the left side of the car, I noticed the steering wheel was on the other side. I had never considered that I would have to drive from the opposite side of the car and on the opposite side of the road. Everything was a first: traveling solo, being in Scotland, and of course, steering from the right while driving on the left. My journey had just begun.

I was totally unprepared for the sheer terror that followed. Each time a car approached mine, my body reacted like I was about to have a head-on collision. Gripping the wheel of the stick shift car, I muttered, "Stay to the left, Jane. Stay to the left." I was learning the importance of remaining focused on what was going on around me. I had no choice. My usual strong Scottish warrior self wanted to cry tears of frustration, but I didn't dare risk blurring my vision.

As I gripped the wheel in near-panic, I had my first Celtic angel track, evidence of my guardian angels. Before leaving home, I had printed directions to my first night's destination, St. Andrews. Of course, they were useless when I couldn't take my eyes off the road and wasn't able to see signs or a place to pull over and ask for help. So I did what any logical person would do—I kept driving straight with my eyes glued to the street. While coasting through a town as school was letting out, I had my first, deeply felt prayer on Scottish soil. "God, please don't let me hit any of these rosy-cheeked kids!"

At that moment, I felt I had no control over my life and was moving forward on an angel wing and a prayer. A couple of hours later, I was able to look up. The first sign I saw read, "St. Andrews straight ahead." It was a wink from my angels. To this day, I do not know how I got there, especially after retracing my drive on the map. Really. What are the odds I got to where I needed to go without following a map? This was a hint of how I would be living my life from now on.

Author Eckhart Tolle wrote, "Realize deeply that the present moment is all you ever have." (*The Power of Now: A Guide to Spiritual Enlightenment*, 35) In other words, "Jane, get out of your head." Staying aware of my surroundings helped me do just that. Hanging onto the edge of the abyss of my long illness, I lived one day at a time just to survive. When necessary, I broke it down to one hour at a time and even ten-minute increments. This discipline stopped me from feeling self-pity and desperation, assuming a bleak future, and spiraling into depression. I did not spend time in the past nor dare to dream of a future. The now—today—was the critical focus during my crisis.

Once steadier on my feet and assured of surviving, I was able to shift out of my one-day-at-a-time crisis mode to observe what was happening around me and be more proactive. I monitored myself closely—my thoughts, my diet, and my reactions to others. I noted how my body responded. Better or worse? Energized or deflated? This information had been available to me all along. Modern day warrior Nancy M.

Turcich fell from a forty-foot cliff and suffered paralysis. Through continual monitoring, she transformed her body into an excellent teacher and her best healing partner. Nancy is a model to me. (Chapter 30, A Walking Miracle)

The present is also the only time I can make a change in my life. I can adjust my attitude (be positive and not give up). I can alter my viewpoint (see the good that comes from an experience). I can practice patience (have faith that Heavenly Team Jane has better timing than I do). I can adopt self-compassion (remind myself that I am doing my best). I came up with a plan to make these disciplines a habit.

First, I had to resign from being a professional worrier. I had believed if I could identify, analyze, and plan for every conceivable, unfavorable outcome, then I was prepared for the future. It took a lot of time and energy—and I had neither to spare due to chronic fatigue syndrome (CFS)—to invent stressful and unlikely situations beyond my control. I could control how I responded to what was going on around me in the moment. Then, I devoted my efforts to consciously noticing people and things around me, scanning my body for how I felt, and observing my actions. I dealt with reality, ending my intense disconnection from what was happening around me. I came out of my head.

Being present was becoming a habit, and going to Scotland alone helped make it happen. I was a one-woman band in a foreign land with unfamiliar customs. I was driver, navigator, bell captain, and sometimes cook. My ability to stay in the now grew stronger with each visit.

I am no longer as distracted as I once was by that negative, noisy voice in my head. It was an obstacle to my healing. Living in the moment has helped me become more mindful. I am receiving better information and making better decisions about my health. I am more aware of what is possible. Change. Healing. Miracles. I pause for reflection, search for the good, and acknowledge my wins. I am amazed at how many miracles I had forgotten. I only need to stay present and keep my eyes on the road.

3

Leaving My Comfort Zones
The Blob

N ot again!" Looking at a photograph from my most recent trip to
Scotland, I saw a thick, bright white blob outlined in red near
the base of a castle ruin. I am physically repelled. It took a full-blown
case of the heebie-jeebies for Heavenly Team Jane to finally get my
attention. I needed to leave the comfort zone that was blocking my
healing.

I had seen similar images in my travel photographs from other Scotland trips, and I easily dismissed each. It was "just the angle of the sun"
or "my camera." But my body never reacted like this before. To check
myself, I took out my stack of pictures from prior trips and shuffled
through them like a deck of playing cards. As I suspected, a light appeared in a picture from every trip to Scotland. Really. What are the
odds? These images captured only on film must mean something.

On Iona, an island in western Scotland, fuzzy white lines come
straight at me.

On an Orkney island, a red mist surrounds a medieval ruin.

En route to Scotland near Blenheim Palace in England, a skeleton
wearing a blue bishop's hat and a pink Casper-the-Friendly-Ghost
shape are above a Doyle tombstone.

At Schiehallion, known as the "Fairy Hill of the Caledonians," a
rectangle of white light hovers over my chest and head.

I tested a selection of the photographs on others. They were amazed
by the earlier images, but each got the willies from the most recent one
with the red-bordered glow. Our identical reactions confirmed what I
had suspected. Something was there. I was not imagining it. Finally,

Heavenly Team Jane had gotten my attention by using the Blob.

When I took the pictures, I never noticed any unusual light—unlike when you see a rainbow and recognize it and feel excited and want to take its picture. I never saw any forms of light while touring Scotland. Later looking at the photograph of the Blob, my brain again said the camera was defective, but this time my emotions knew the truth. I whispered, "Woo woo!" Woo woo is my term for a supernatural event beyond ordinary experience and scientific explanation. This aha moment validated woo woo to me. Seeing is believing, but maybe not seeing could be believing too. Maybe something doesn't have to be proven to be perceived as real.

My new belief was a tidal wave. For over half a century, in public, I had stayed within a traditional comfort zone. In private, I read books about woo woo. My encounter with the Blob made it real, and finally, my conservative shell started to crack. I was stepping out of the closet spiritually. It may not sound like much, but moving through this fear changed my life. I could now pursue non-traditional health treatments.

My definition of leaving a comfort zone is doing something I fear. I dreaded being exposed as someone drawn to the mystical realm. I was certain that my peers would disapprove if they found out I was intrigued by all religions, sacred sites, and energy medicine. And now, I was a woo woo believer who sees blobs in her vacation pictures. I kept mum. By hiding a part of myself, resisting change, and staying with what was familiar—even if ineffective, I prolonged my suffering and ruined my health.

With Heavenly Team Jane's encouragement, I had been building a track record of firsts, starting with my initial trip to Scotland. I was ready when my clever guides used magical Scotland as my woo woo training ground. My crew convinced me that the unexplained—the auras of light and everything else—was real. I could not have imagined these experiences had I tried.

And yet, I was still playing it safe. My cloak of anonymity as a tourist was my armor in Scotland. I told few people back in the States about my experiences, but confided in no one about my conversion to being a card-carrying Christian spiritualist. That is why I am inspired by how quickly Arlene Faulk, a modern day warrior firmly rooted in Western medicine, moved out of her comfort zone and embraced the world of alternative remedies. (Chapter 24, A Gentle Reminder) What happened when I finally emerged from my shell? Well, to quote Sir William Wallace from the movie *Braveheart*: "Freedom!" I was free to consider different treatments.

As in most new endeavors, I experienced roadblocks and stormy weather along the way. I tested the waters by telling one trusted person (my sister Susie in Alabama). Then I retreated back into my shell and sought help from Heavenly Team Jane. With their encouragement and by staying in the moment, I could persevere. I also gained energy from Scotland's sacred sites. I made it through and emerged stronger.

When God wants me to move to the next level or take another step on my life's journey, a comfort zone is disrupted. God sure disrupted mine with health issues. The more courage required, the wider my stride became. Like Winston Churchill said, "This is no time for ease and comfort. It is time to dare and endure." And that is what I did. I shook things up by traveling to Scotland alone.

My courage was fueled in the aftermath of 9/11. Realizing life's too short, I packed my bags for Scotland. Focusing on the journey (life's brevity) instead of the destination (Scotland) helped me move forward. My first big stride was that trip to Scotland. Had I known then it would mean six years of reprogramming my life, I probably would have said "no thank-you" and cancelled my reservation. But all I knew was that life was passing me by because of my illnesses, and it was time I enjoy myself.

Now I remain flexible and do not try to control—or even assume—the outcome of life changes, especially when leaving a comfort zone.

My intended destination may not be known at the outset. In other words, it may not be what I packed my bags for. I have faith that Heavenly Team Jane will lead me to where I need to be.

I am glad I jumped into my fear. I agree with George Carlin, "Life's journey is not meant to arrive at the grave safely in a well preserved body, but rather to skid in sideways, totally worn out, and shouting, "Holy cow. What a ride!" And perhaps with a blob of light trailing close behind.

4

Seeing the Good

Good Dragons

Here be dragons!" I muttered the medieval phrase for danger as I scurried back to my rental car in Findhorn, the spiritual community and learning center in northern Scotland. Earlier, I had congratulated myself on being comfortable with the unexplainable by not moving out of the house when I saw a ghost (my first). I thought I had this woo woo stuff conquered until I drove to Findhorn that day and walked into its bookshop. I smelled something that made me uncomfortable. I was out of there. Pronto. My knee-jerk reaction taught me there is value in everything that happens, especially the frightening. Even dragons. Sometimes it takes a while to find the good, but it is always there.

Once home, I became curious why I had hightailed it out of the there. I did my research, and learned that many influential speakers were on the events calendar at Findhorn. Seeing this made me feel safe enough to return, and I went right back to the bookshop.

As I entered the store, I smelled the same strong odor that I had before. My calmer state of mind realized that I smelled church. I smelled incense. My church at home and the bookshop burned similar incense. Hmm. Was my initial flight out of the store a reaction to my fear of the non-traditional meeting the conventional? Were two vital parts of myself—my fascination with the spiritual and my religious devotion—playing hide-and-seek with each other?

This time when I smelled the incense, I did not run. I stayed. I browsed. I bought some books and even a piece of art. Then I ventured outside and followed a path around the grounds. After climbing a small mound, I had another unusual Scottish experience. From my toes to my head, I felt waves of fabulous sensation. I sat down on a nearby tree stump and cried tears of joy. Yep. In my journal, I described the powerful happening under the heading "Another Mystical Woo Woo Event Unsolved."

Had I not been spooked during my first visit to the Findhorn center, I may not have researched it. And my eyes may not have opened to a new world: alternative medicine. It had never occurred to me the spiritual community could offer a health component, that it was more than campfire stories of things that go bump in the night. Further, I was able to reconcile within myself that the unconventional and the conventional could be harnessed for the purpose of healing. For the first time, I connected the dots. Jane the Apprentice saw the good.

My return visit confirmed the benefit of what I call hitting a "false bottom." Several years before I went to Scotland, I thought my health couldn't get any worse, but it did. Hello, false bottom. Now, I see the good that came from the further decline. If it had been a real bottom and I recovered, I would have been the same old Jane without any pain. I would not have traversed Scotland tip to tip, met my heavenly team, stepped out of the closet spiritually, and become Jane the Apprentice learning to self-heal. I would have left new skills, greater knowledge, and waves of pleasure in the closet (or on a mound in Findhorn). I love bottoms—false or real—because good inevitably follows.

My pain and suffering continued and at times, were debilitating. By persevering, I uncovered the value of each experience. After years of focusing on my agonies, was it easy to see the good? Absolutely not. And certainly not when collapsing into bed at six each night and gritting my teeth. Curled up in misery, I was not smiling through any pain. But I could hum Al Green's "Everything's Gonna Be Alright" and look forward to the day when I would see the good.

Then my perception changed. I had two choices on how to live my life: the easy way or the hard way. And I was tired of living life the hard way. At the beginning of my health struggles, I was stuck in fear and chose not to change (the hard way). When I relied on wiser powers, Heavenly Team Jane, the wild colt within me tamed. I began to discover and live as the true Jane (the easy way).

To live my life the easy way, I became accountable for everything that happens to me in my life. No more of the blame game. I choose my thoughts, words, and deeds carefully. As Epictetus said, "It is not what happens to you, but how you react." I agree.

Much good came from the hurricanes in my life. They dawned with my health issues and ignited my emotional fears. I became socially isolated and financially insecure. And now was I on the menu for a dragon? I doubted everything. The insignificant part of me blew away and uncovered the core of who I was, not what others wanted me to be. I felt purified by a super laundry detergent for the @#%! in my life.

These storms were Heavenly Team Jane's invitation for a happier life. I had a strong knowing that if I accepted the forces in my life instead of resisting, I would irrevocably change into a new Jane—one I could not have imagined. I envisioned myself as a tree firmly rooted during a ferocious hurricane. I could resist and break or go with the flow and become a different person. I chose to bend.

As Al Green predicted, everything did end up alright. Even better than alright. My road back to health was the most rewarding of my life (so far). Along the way, fueled by each accomplishment, I felt snippets of joy. It doesn't get much better for me.

British novelist C. S. Lewis said, "Hardship often prepares an ordinary person for an extraordinary destiny." Maybe Lewis was spot-on, and something extraordinary was happening to me. The possibility inspired me to be a detective for the good in my life.

My Findhorn experiences were perfect. They put a spotlight on my biggest fear blocking recovery. I could not get well until I faced my intrigue with the unconventional. Non-traditional communities could offer opportunities to heal. I saw the good. I whisper, "Here be dragons!" and then, I find the good one.

5

Listening to My Body

A Rock-Solid Relationship

I was sitting in my bed-and-breakfast in the beautiful village of Killin. I had just read the local legend of Saint Fillan's healing stones. My intuition kept calling out to me. "Jane, go hold the rocks!" Of course, I wondered why I should go to the effort to find fourteen hundred-year-old rocks. With my usual headache, after driving hours and finally arriving at my B and B, I was exhausted. But Heavenly Team Jane would not give up. I called Killin's Tweed Mill, home of the famous healing stones, and was told that the next day was one of the few dates in February with visiting hours. Really. What are the odds that I am in this small Highland village over one of the few winter days Tweed Mill is open? I was about to be introduced to a valuable and reliable healing partner: my body.

The next morning I stood in front of a small collection of rocks placed on a bed of straw in the back corner. My intuition again persisted, "Pick them up, Jane. Hold the rocks!" I thought, "Are you crazy? I'll end up in a Scottish jail accused of attempted robbery of a national treasure." So I did what any logical American tourist would do. Turning to the lady at the reception desk, I asked, "May I touch the rocks?" She not only said "yes," but also encouraged me.

The kind lady shared the legend of the healing stones. Saint Fillan came to Killin around the end of the seventh century. He was a follower of the famous Saint Columba, the Irish monk credited with having brought Christianity to Scotland. The stones were used to heal people back then and are said to be healing people still today.

That was all I needed to hear. I reached down with my right hand

and picked up the nearest stone. My hand began to tingle. Then, I picked up another stone and felt the same tingling sensation in my head. The lady continued her explanation. Each rock is particularly effective at healing a specific body part. Typically, people hold the rocks and rub them on the part in pain. The stones are believed to have cured everything from headaches to hearing and vision loss. Hold on. Did she say "headaches"? I thought of my aching head and asked, "Headaches? Which rock?"

I found it fascinating that the legend was still alive after all those years and interesting that my headache improved. I dismissed the thoughts as I left Tweed Mill. I got back in my car and headed farther west towards my original destination (where I had planned to go before learning about Saint Fillan's healing rocks): Iona, the home of Saint Columba, the man Saint Fillan admired. Hmm. A coincidence? An angel track telling me to not so quickly write off my experience with the healing rocks?

I may have consciously dismissed the Scottish moment of energy coursing through my hand and head, but not subconsciously. Over a decade later, the sensation is clear as a bell. Something stuck. Since that day, I have been drawn to collect stones and investigate their healing properties. I have set gems into jewelry. I sleep on a Richway's Amethyst BioMat, and my leg cramps are gone. I purchased a set of overhead lamps containing crystals, which rejuvenates me.

Yes, something awoke inside me when I held Saint Fillan's healing rocks. I became curious. If my body reacted to the stones by tingling, maybe it responds to other things, too—such as people, food, places, and my emotions. I became a student of my body. Over time, this proved to be correct. My physical body had been giving me valuable, honest feedback all along. I began to listen closely.

I feel drained by some people, and more energetic with others.

I get gas from eating certain foods, and I feel more alive and energetic drinking freshly juiced vegetables.

I naturally gravitate to devotional places where prayers are spoken. At the Musée de Cluny in Paris, I walked into a room and was drawn to lay on the bench. I later read that the room had once been part of a medieval monastery. I love the energy of prayers.

When I am angry, my body feels drained. When I am in love, I feel the whole world is in love with me.

My body and I may have gotten off to a rocky start, but I now recognize it as my most reliable, vocal friend, with no hidden agendas and my best interests at heart. Before I held Saint Fillan's rocks, if someone had asked me if I had a relationship with my body, I would have said, "Yes. Absolutely. A rocky one. Perhaps even an antagonistic one." My body seemed to delight in torturing me with physical and emotional pain. Now, I understand my error in judgment. I took the long, hard way to realize that the true source of pain is my body's 9-1-1 call for help. My body uses pain to yell, "Stop that;" discomfort to warn, "That's not healthy;" and pleasure to purr, "Atta girl, Jane."

Then, I began to wonder if I was bringing on my symptoms via the Law of Attraction (that is, like attracts like). Was I bringing on my agony by assuming that I would be in pain each day? Was my body responding to my expectation of pain? After all, my first thought every morning upon opening my eyes was "where do I hurt?" It was time for an experiment. I simply changed my morning thought to "where do I feel good?" Over time, my symptoms began to lessen—proof positive that my body was listening to my new thought pattern.

This seemingly small test—replacing one word in my morning self-talk—caused a cosmic shift in my thoughts. If my body was listening to me, maybe I could take it a step further. Could I tell my body what I needed and how I wanted to feel? Could I establish a two-way communication system with my body and create what I wanted?

I started watching the words coming out of my mouth and my silent thoughts. I frequently used the words "fear" and "scared," emotional states that I am not interested in attracting. I broke the habit by repeating aloud words that represent my desired state: "Joy. Joy. Joy." When I woke up rested but with low energy, I said, "My intent is to have lots and lots of energy." My body listened, proving that my words and thoughts are powerful and it's important to choose them carefully. Just like how modern day warrior L. A. thought about the word "harmony," and her body responded and pancreas healed. Yes, words are powerful. (Chapter 19, My Mother Would Not Have Recognized Me)

I later consulted with the Scottish medical doctor David Mickel. He encouraged me to keep a log of when my symptoms flared and my emotions at the time. This tool was a real eye-opener and helped me discern significant patterns. It also revealed a meaningful blind spot that Dr. Mickel saw early on, but I had shrugged off. With the deeper insights, I was able to refine my dialogue with my body and do so with positive results.

My body is more than an alert system; we are a call-and-response team to wellness. I hear my body, and my body hears me. I still have trouble translating my body's cues and can be slow understanding the meaning of certain aches and pains (my ankle once ached for months before I learned it needed realignment). I leave several blank lines in my unique healing formula, my wellness plan, for new conditions that my body will want to bring to my attention. The body will never give up on me.

The most beautiful people we have known are those who have known defeat, known suffering, known struggle, known loss, and have found their way out of the depths. These persons have an appreciation, a sensitivity, and an understanding of life that fills them with compassion, gentleness, and a deep loving concern. Beautiful people do not just happen. (Elisabeth Kübler-Ross, *Death: The Final Stage of Growth*, 96)

Just think. If I had not picked up Saint Fillan's rocks, I would not have felt the physical sensations or the validation when my headache improved. I would not have discovered what an amazing self-healing partner my body can be. I intend to build on my past experiences by nurturing our rock-solid relationship. Our strong alliance is how I can be my most sparkly, beautiful self. A gem unto myself.

6

Pausing, but Never Giving Up
A Fair-Weathered Angel

Standing on the rocky western shore of Scotland overlooking the Irish Sea, I yelled, "Archangel Michael!" and stomped my right foot in frustration. My passionate plea from deep within surprised even me. And why Michael, that great warrior angel? Regardless, it worked. Suddenly, the howling wind stopped, the drizzling rain stopped, and the sun came out. But it was not the weather that had this Southern American girl's panties in a wad. It was what happened to me as I was walking to the cave of Scotland's first saint, Saint Ninian.

You see, I had had it. It was my fifth trip to Scotland, in 2005, and I was bombarded by fears. My prayers weren't helping, and I was at the end of my rope. My interaction with Archangel Michael that day in Scotland gave me insight into my life's journey. I learned why it is important to stay the course even when I make a wrong turn, to pause and recharge my batteries but never give up.

Walking the wooded path to the oceanside cave, I was overcome by irrational fears. "Here be dragons! And they're real." This walk was among the many mystical, unexplainable events that I had during my six years of visits to Scotland as Jane the Apprentice. You may find the rapid weather change, a miracle to me, hard to believe. I would have doubted it myself had it not happened to me. So I don't blame you, although I will remind you of my definition of a miracle. Something you believe is impossible becomes possible. I was convinced of this truth. I hung a photograph of St. Ninian's Cave that I took that day. It reminds me that miracles really do happen and can happen to me. Thank goodness I persevered, or I would not have experienced one of the most memorable events of my life and gotten to know Archangel Michael.

I was visiting Whithorn, the town of the first recorded Christian church in Scotland, built by Saint Ninian around 397 AD (I love early medieval history) and had just seen the sign "St. Ninian's Cave this way." I got the nudge for an adventure. It was a typical Scottish February day—overcast with a slight drizzle. "So, why not?"

I parked my car and followed the sign pointing into the woods. Scotland has great signage. In the United States, frequent signs remind us we are on the right track. Not so in this Celtic country. They have one sign that you are on the correct path, and you are expected to keep going straight until you get to another sign to change directions. This gut-loving woman, learning to thrive on adventures, had come to enjoy the Scots' effective-without-coddling directions. They enabled me to practice staying the course by checking in with my intuition. I am used to being told every couple of miles that I am on the right course. In Scotland, I had to intuit it. I gleefully start my newest adventure.

I came to a fork in the wooded path, and there was no sign. What? My theory was busted. After working through my confusion, I decided to go right and came to a stream. I saw that the path continued on the other side of the water, but decided not to cross. I had already been slipping on the wet leaves and did not want to get my tennis shoes wetter. (Later, I realized that there was probably no sign because both paths took you to St. Ninian's Cave. The Scots didn't let me down after all.) I backtracked to the fork in the road, and thus began my trail of terror.

I saw a sign: "Beware of bulls." A spike of panic pierced my heart. I tried to calm down by reminding myself that the sign was on the other side of a fence. Unless bulls can jump fences, I should be OK. Still rattled, I moved on. Then, I saw a snake at my feet (snakes are one of my biggest fears). I was paralyzed with fear. Upon further examination, I saw that the snake was a stick.

It was irrational, but I was still rattled. I started praying and kept on walking. My next thought was that I was going to slip on the wet leaves, twist my ankle, and be stranded in a deserted forest. I rationalized that yes, it was possible but unlikely. "Just watch where you step, Jane." My prayers intensified. Up ahead, among the trees, I saw the ocean. The end was in sight. I kept walking.

Suddenly, the wind picked up, the rain started, and I didn't have an umbrella. That's it. I am done with being wracked by fears. I was angry. And that was when, without a thought, I exploded into the tantrum, "Archangel Michael!" and stomped my right foot. Immediately, the wind died, the rain stopped, and the sun came out. The shift was so sudden, as if God flipped a light switch. I was stunned. I can't explain it. I have no idea why my soul chose Archangel Michael to come to my rescue. But he did. Ever since, I have had an affinity for that great warrior angel.

I arrived at St. Ninian's Cave. I saw a father with his young son and overheard him say, "It's time to leave." He must have heard me yell and wanted to protect his innocent child from this mad American woman. My pockets were full of rocks as mementos, and I felt dazed. I spent some time in the ancient hermitage. And then, I walked rapidly back to my car.

As soon as I shut the car door, the sun hid behind big clouds, the wind picked up, and the drizzle started again. The weather changed abruptly, just like when I had stomped my right foot. The second sudden shift was confirmation that something special had just happened. Really. What are the odds? It felt like a metaphor of my life—my health struggles were the trail of terror. I needed to get back to my B and B and call my sister Susie in Alabama. I assumed she would not believe the miracle, but she did.

I am grateful that I did not give up. Not at the fork in the road. Not at the stream. Not at the sign warning of bulls. Not by my mirage of a snake. Not at my premonition of a twisted ankle. Not by stormy weather. Not once did I walk back to my car and drive away. Instead, each time, I paused. And then, I cried out for help from the heavens.

Had I given up, I would not have experienced the weather miracles. I would not have learned the power of Archangel Michael, a new member of Heavenly Team Jane. I would not have known the help of Heavenly Team Jane with my life's struggles and even crises. Not giving up can be life changing, as modern day warrior Breck Pappas did with an act of kindness. (Chapter 21, Fake It till You Make It)

Many people with good intentions tried to discourage me from finding a cure to my undiagnosed illnesses. Their warnings to spare me disappointment were a trap that I needed to avoid. My intuition's deep wisdom, Heavenly Team Jane's persistent nudges, helps me stay the course and never give up. When things get tough and I am about to give up, I am inspired by my walk to St. Ninian's Cave. I remember Archangel Michael's weather wand, and I carry on. I know firsthand miracles lay on the other side of struggles. The sunny side.

PART II.

Jane the Explorer
(2009–2012)

I am an enthusiast for all things spiritual. But I was closeted until Labor Day 2008. On that day, I stepped a toe outside of this comfort zone to attend an alternative conference in Mount Shasta, California. I went to consult a Scottish doctor about my chronic fatigue syndrome (CFS). My previous travels throughout Scotland fine-tuned my sense of adventure and gave me the tools to turn situations around. I was more proactive and open to new ideas. Now, to heal myself once again, I was packing for a solo trip. But this time, the destination was beyond my sanctuary of safety. Heavenly Team Jane re-issued my passport in the name of Jane the Explorer.

For years, I had a persistent knowing that my CFS was curable despite common belief about the disorder, but I lacked the energy to pursue it until summer 2008. Heavenly Team Jane prodded me to google "chronic fatigue syndrome cure." In a few months, the Scottish doctor David Mickel was traveling to the United States to present his behavior-based treatment for conditions including CFS.

Really. What are the odds the conference was sponsored by the geologist James Tipton, with whom I was corresponding privately about his travels to sacred sites? What are the odds of this impeccable timing on the heels of my six-year love affair with Scotland and right before Dr. Mickel's trip to America? What are the odds I would find a Scottish doctor? What are the odds Dr. Mickel was a conservatively trained doctor, a comfort to me since I was using only Western physicians at that point? The angel tracks got this conventional girl with unconventional interests to take a first step out of the closet. Then, I received a confirming angel wink. James Tipton is married to a Scottish woman. Yes, Heavenly Team Jane was making sure I saw this opportunity through my love for that Celtic country.

Heavenly Team Jane dangled three carrots before me: my desire to be cured of CFS, a correspondent I had grown to respect, and a traditional medical doctor from my beloved Scotland. With renewed hope, I was determined to do whatever it took to cure my CFS. At the conference, I had my first appointment with Dr. Mickel. I saw immediate improvements with his self-help technique, and we continued working together. My success gave me confidence to consider other health conditions that had made me feel like Humpty Dumpty, where no one was able to put me back together again.

Dr. Mickel was a major turning point in my healing journey, and others I met through James Tipton were stepping stones. They exposed me to a new world of healing called "energy medicine" and were the healing bridge connected me to the Brazilian spiritual healer known as the "Miracle Man." What are the odds that over the next three months, I continually heard about this Miracle Man? April 2009, I followed these angel tracks and leaped into the unknown. I landed in Brazil. My perspective of this world (and myself) changed forever.

At the Casa healing center, I made three important realizations.

- I had been consulting and relying on the wrong king and king's men (like Humpty Dumpty had) for answers, because it is God— that great universal force of love—who can do anything.
- The only limitations God has is what we place on God.
- Miracles exist.

After that first trip to Brazil in 2009, I left believing in miracles but only those that happened to others. After my second trip the following year, I believed miracles could also happen to me. I had hope. Maybe my doctors were wrong. I left as Jane the Explorer. I became passionate about searching for miracles, self-healing stories, my personal remedies, and other inspirational examples.

If my intuition endorsed it, no matter how far-fetched it seemed to me, I would go exploring. I traveled the world. I heard accounts of physical, emotional, and spiritual healing in the United States, Europe, Canada, North Africa, Latin America, and the Middle East. Some favorites are Salar de Uyuni in Bolivia, Jerusalem, the Great Sphinx of Giza in Egypt, and Mont Saint-Michel in Normandy and Lourdes in France. My soundest sleep was at the natural hot springs in Banff, Canada. I perused the library of Edgar Cayce, the late medical clairvoyant and a father of holistic medicine, in Virginia Beach, Virginia. I met paranormal investigators, near-death survivors, and plant medicine doctors. Trying it all, Jane the Explorer busted out of her comfort zone in a big way.

I have tested dozens of healing remedies and techniques, some of which have yet to be embraced by Western medicine but are helping people in other parts of the world. I experimented with prayer, colonics, Kineseo taping, crystal healing beds, Tesla's Violet Ray Therapy, HcG (human chorionic gonadotropin) diet, reflexology, juicing vegetables, Aim Emc vibration therapy, Marnitz soft tissue therapy, rolfing, intuitive healing, homeopathic energy medicine, sweat lodge purification, sound therapy, yoga, hypnotherapy, Himalayan salt treatments, and more. Some worked for me. Others didn't. That's one of the joys of being an explorer: discovery with an open mind and no expectations.

Christopher Columbus said, "You can never cross the ocean unless you have the courage to lose sight of the shore." I did that when I went to Brazil. For the next seven years, I opened my heart and mind, packed a suitcase, and searched for my unique healing formula. As Jane the Explorer, I took five more steps on my stairway to joy.

Expecting My Miracles. Instead of witnessing God's miracles for others, expecting my own launched my adventures as Jane the Explorer. A stranger's penetrating gaze was my signal to the countdown. (Chapter 7, The Gaze)

Taking Responsibility. Back at the Casa, a sea of rejected prescriptions reminded me to do my part. I became a modern day warrior to rescue myself. (Chapter 8, Back in the Saddle)

Investing in Myself. During my health crisis, I saw how expenses can soar and income can plummet. I developed a litmus test to help me ease my fears. (Chapter 9, If Money Were No Object)

Finding My Healing Partners. An angel track during my fifth trip to Brazil inspired me to find the best fit in a practitioner. Answers to Jane's Olympics Tryout Checklist refined the search, and I had my ideal team. (Chapter 10, Jane's Olympians)

Creating My Unique Healing Formula. Leaving Brazil one spring, I decided no more pain. As if on a treasure hunt, I discovered my personalized blend of healing partners, treatments, and practices. (Chapter 11, "Freedom!")

My adventures are a rush of excitement, but you don't have to go to Brazil to discover your inner warrior. You can stay at home and explore your remedy and rescue yourself. All you need is the courage to lose sight of the shore, and arrive at a new world of wellness.

7

Expecting My Miracles
The Gaze

"May I join you?" the handsome gentleman asked. My dinner companions and I smiled and nodded yes. It was my second trip to Abadiânia, Brazil, home of the spiritual healer Joao de Deus. The stranger sat down and told us his healing story while looking directly at me. His gaze put me on high alert. I was about to receive confirmation of my belief that God can do anything. The only limitation God has is what we place on God.

The stranger was a European-trained doctor descended from a long line of physicians. He was dying of cancer and had had seven unsuccessful operations. His major organs were shutting down—some functioning at only a quarter capacity. About to give up, he saw a Discovery Channel television special on the Casa. Despite his family legacy and traditional education, he was drawn to visit this miracle man in Brazil. And he did. After several trips to Abadiânia, he could go home. He was healed.

The stranger's story inspired me to believe that maybe I, a conservative, middle-aged American from the Deep South, could experience my own miracles. My first trip to Brazil a year earlier, I saw miracles happened in modern times, but considered they happened only to others. Now I believed that God could heal my impossible situation. Although I did not have cancer and was not a doctor, I identified with my fellow traveler. I, too, had deteriorating health. I, too, received no cure from traditional medicine. I, too, had almost given up hope when I heard of the spiritual healer and came to Brazil.

***

After my last trip to Scotland, I eased out of the closet spiritually by attending an alternative conference in Mount Shasta, California. I kept hearing about a man who calls himself "Joao de Deus" because God (Deus)—not he—does the healing. I went to my computer and googled him. *"The Book of Miracles: The Healing Work of Joao de Deus* by Josie RavenWing" popped up. I ordered the book. While I read that someone should go for an extended stay at the healing center, my overhead lights flickered off and on. It was an in-my-face angel track, my personal Discovery Channel special. As an angel wink, I later learned that Dr. David Mickel, the Scottish physician who helped cure my chronic fatigue syndrome, had also visited.

Three months later, I arrived for a two-week visit. I returned home in awe of God's handiwork: miracles. I witnessed what I believed was impossible. It was as if the Bible came alive. In this small town in Brazil, once-crippled people could walk. Once-blind people could see. And a man who had been dying of cancer was going home healed. What I had thought was impossible became possible: my definition of a miracle. All along, I had been the only one limiting myself—not God. The world I had embraced for over half a century fell apart.

I started to rebuild my foundation. By bringing God into my Humpty Dumpty dilemma, I had found my correct king and all the king's horses and all the king's men. By expecting my miracles, I had finally begun to receive answers, recapture my life, and live new dreams. Heavenly Team Jane nudged me into action with the European doctor's story, as with the Blob in my Scotland photographs that inspired me to move outside of my comfort zone. (Chapter 3, The Blob) I love angel tracks.

I came home from Brazil wondering if others felt the same way, and so I polled my peers. "How do you define 'a miracle'?" "Have you ever experienced one?"

Many, like I had, believed in miracles but didn't think they could happen to them. Others didn't believe in miracles at all. A couple believed in miracles and experienced them regularly. Some responses raised my eyebrows, and a few made me think, "Wow. Really?" Definitions were different, just like every person is unique. Among the definitions, I discovered one ingredient of creating miracles—putting the needs of others before our own. Modern day warrior P. J. D. did that and began to heal from alcoholism. (Chapter 15, Jiminy Cricket)

Some people may question my miraculous healings and imply I was misdiagnosed. Maybe, maybe not. More importantly, it doesn't matter what anyone else thinks. Only what I think. No one can take my miracle away from me. Thus, my definition of a miracle is: when something you—and even if only you—believed impossible becomes possible.

Miracles may be unique, but they're not rare. God's healing power is everywhere. Miracles can be found in churches and hospitals; a healer's touch, words of wisdom, and prayer; plants and food; a hug. I suspect in other ways, too, that I have yet to explore. Miracles are accessible to everyone.

Once I acknowledged miracles, I saw them everywhere. They come in all shapes and sizes, every day, and to everyone. They happen regardless of one's illness, age, gender, race, religion, and nationality—not only to special and blessed people, but also to others like me. They were always there for me to see and embrace. I only had to believe and to open my eyes.

Expecting my miracles became like chasing the American dream, a vivid ideal from my childhood. We could achieve anything with focus and hard work. So, in the spirit of the American dream, I decided to go for it. I made a list of all the miracles I wanted and checked it twice. Some miracles have materialized, and some have yet to materialize. Others didn't turn out as expected; they turned out better. That is the magic of miracles. They often surprise you.

Searching for miracles as Jane the Explorer was my second chance at life and how I healed myself. Matthew, one of Jesus's twelve apostles, said, "Ask, and it shall be given to you." (Matt. 7:7). I would add, "And doing ye part by searching for your miracles and welcoming a stranger to sit at your table."

8

Taking Responsibility

Back in the Saddle

Hundreds of pieces of paper were strewn across the ground at a Casa event. Unfilled prescriptions—missed opportunities to heal—had been tossed away. My tour guide was disheartened. For the past two decades, she had seen the wonders and healings that came from these herbs energized for each person's specific request. Our conversation triggered the aha thought: Was I taking advantage of all opportunities in my life and in particular, my healing? Was I discarding them like a used tissue? I was inspired to examine ways I could take more responsibility.

It was always my choice whether or not to accept recommendations. And if I had chosen to follow the advice of my physicians, why wouldn't I do the same with God (via Joao de Deus)? I committed to faithfully follow the guidance. When I received my slip of paper for herbs, I filled it and kept refilling it for the next five years. My herbs were the staple of my recovery.

Why did some people choose to discard their recommendations? Was it financial? Could they not afford to fill their prescriptions? The cost is minimal by American standards and even free for those with economic challenges. Perhaps they expected someone else to heal them, like I had done for decades. In Brazil, I was told people contribute to their illnesses by their actions, and that if we don't do our part, the symptoms will likely return. That made sense to me.

Giving my doctors complete control over my health (without validation from my intuition) was one of my biggest missteps. I had a lot more control over my life and wellness than I imagined. I committed myself to becoming the cowgirl steering my herd of healing partners and to be fully accountable for the results. Eleanor Roosevelt said, "In the long run, we shape our lives, and we shape ourselves. The process never ends until we die. And the choices we make are ultimately our own responsibility." Well said, Eleanor.

Taking responsibility helped me finally change my childhood habit of following the pack. I had let others persuade me, even for mundane things. If I wanted to see a particular movie and asked a friend to join me, she would agree but invite others along. Next thing I knew, I was watching a movie that I did not want to see with people I did not necessarily enjoy. I needed to change my actions, but chose not to move out of the comfort zone of not offending anyone (even if that meant not speaking my truth). I was electing against doing my part.

By default, I was allowing others to make decisions for me. My friends were not trying to be unkind; I just had a herd mentality. I grazed the landscape aimlessly, like how I would one day manage my wellness. My body had to revolt to get my attention. It communicated loud and clear, "Jane, become a cowgirl and take the reins."

Taking responsibility was part of my treatment. To heal, I needed to help myself and not just rely on God and the rest of Heavenly Team Jane. My job was to move on their suggestions and not throw away their prescriptions. I could no longer be a wandering steer. I am inspired by how modern day warrior Yorli Huff took charge and wrote her own prescription to cure injustice. (Chapter 16, Choose a Positive Outcome)

I became accountable for the daily headaches I had had for thirty years. If I could change my childhood habit of following the herd and reduce my pain, what else could I tackle in my life? Could I stop people from hurting me? Had I been the one wounding myself by allowing others to hurt me? No one could hurt my feelings unless I allowed them to get to me. No one could make me angry unless I allowed myself to get angry. It was within my control. I was the only one able to stop it.

Taking responsibility for my self-healing does not mean I am alone in the recovery process—although at certain times, I am. Solo in Scotland, I was learning how to be responsible for my actions. I was a one-man band—the driver, navigator, concierge, and tour guide. If something didn't go as planned, I was the one to blame. Lesson learned. I took back the reins. The proof is in the Scottish pudding. In five short years, I healed myself about 90 percent. This cowgirl was back in the saddle.

9

Investing in Myself

If Money Were No Object

I stood in front of a run-down house in Brazil, and saw its potential. The foundation looked solid. How beautiful it would be with just a bit of work. Immediately, I saw a parallel to my physical home—my body. What kind of effort, or investment, was I making to rehab myself? I had given it my all. I spent many hours visiting doctors and even traveled far to consult with those considered the best. I took their recommendations. I consistently took their remedies. And I only got sicker. My materials must have been wrong. I needed to go back to the drawing board.

One of the faulty materials was my attitude toward spending. I have always been a saver. As a kid when I played Monopoly, I hid play money under the game board. As an adult in a health crisis, I panicked when my costs ate into my savings. My fears dictated my every wellness choice. I chose the cheapest option covered by my insurance plan, regardless if it was the best treatment for me.

Standing in front of the Brazilian rehab opportunity, I realized my error. My health expenses were depleting my assets, and I saw no results. Money spent is an investment in me, like fixing up a house. Both investments increase value and enjoyment. It is only a drain when I use the wrong supplies. For example, bricks would not be the best choice to replace a missing log in a cabin.

The reality is, it is expensive to be sick. Costs go up and income goes down when too ill to work full time. Say hello to "the squeeze." It's a time to carefully choose rehab materials. My fear ("I'm gonna run out of money") led me past the custom order desk to the readymade aisle.

My bargain mentality ("It's on sale") replaced my better judgment. And I moved into a money trap. By choosing the wrong treatments based on cost only, I was throwing money down the drain. I needed a litmus test to make the best choice for my health toolbox. When faced with resistance or indecision, I ask myself, "If money were no object, what would I do?"

While in Brazil, I began believing miracles can happen to me. I was determined to do whatever it took to find mine, even if it meant spending my dwindling savings. This inspired me to use the litmus test to ease me out of another comfort zone. I set three intentions to ensure my success. One, I am worth the investment. Two, I committed to actively search for my cures. Three, I will not worry where the money comes from. That's up to Heavenly Team Jane. My wily heavenly helpers responded in surprising ways. Sometimes, I didn't need money because practitioners wanted to develop their skills or gifted me a treatment. My care unfolded perfectly.

After I set my intentions, I needed to do my part by telling Heavenly Team Jane my intention. I had to be patient and open to Heavenly Team Jane's responses. I had to overcome my pride to accept a gift. I had to be fearless and try unfamiliar treatments. I had to be clever like the yogis who worked at the front desk of my studio in exchange for free yoga classes.

Interestingly, when I shifted my stance and saw my efforts as an investment in myself, my income grew. I have a sneaking suspicion it had something to do with trust—my faith in my team, the process, and miracles. Also, as the correct treatments helped me feel better, I became stronger and more productive.

Being prudent with money, especially in times of need, is something I advise. The least expensive route may be the best and most sensible route for the situation. But for me, I wasted a lot of money, time, and energy by not pausing to evaluate the effectiveness of my choices. Ironically, I did exactly what I set out to avoid—waste money. Fear can do that to you. I am not suggesting all medical expenses are a drain on assets, only that the expenses are like the investment to rehab a home. The correct materials and healing partners build the soundest structure.

The success of you healing you is anchored in making the right choices for you. In addition to money, education and time are other ways I invest in me. I learn about treatments curing conditions similar to mine. I respect my body's internal clock instead of imposing a deadline. Modern day warrior Catherine Kominos made a substantial commitment to awaken spiritually. She went on pilgrimages, studied mystical traditions, and dedicated time to practice new disciplines. And it worked. (Chapter 20, Cracking the Safe to My Heart)

Close your eyes, and imagine. You've just been assured that you won't fail at whatever you try, and money is no object. What would your next step in life be?

10

Finding My Healing Partners
Jane's Olympians

During my fifth trip to Brazil, I had an angel track. I met a rolfer, someone trained to manually smooth out fascia (connective tissue in the body). A rolfer releases pain caused by injury, poor posture, and stress. Heavenly Team Jane was nudging me since I suffered from chronic neck and muscular pain. I decided to give this bodywork (known as "rolfing") a try when I got home.

Back to Google I went, and I was immediately drawn to the name of a certified rolfer located near my office. I followed my hunch to Jill Coyne, and it paid off. I found a new (to me) treatment and healing partner knowledgeable about other alternative healing modalities. I saw Jill regularly for one year, and my neck pain was tolerable for the first time in decades. What are the odds a random meeting finally resolved my 24/7 pains?

As Jane the Explorer, I was in the driver's seat but needed committed health-care practitioners like Jill to help me navigate my complex, interrelated conditions. I required a human Heavenly Team Jane in white coats. I used angel tracks to guide me to them.

My sister Susie told me the following story, which fits my definition of a healing partner.

A woman fell down a deep hole and could not figure out how to get out. She tried everything she knew. As a doctor walked by, she yelled, "Help! Help! I'm in the hole! Please help!" The doctor wrote a prescription and threw it in the hole. Then a priest walked by, and hearing the woman's plea for help, threw a prayer in the hole. Then

the woman's friend walked by, saw her in the hole, and jumped in.
The woman asked, "Why did you do that? Now we're both trapped."
The friend said, "Because I've been here before, and I know the way
out." (Author unknown.)

The friend in the story represents my ideal healing partner: someone who has been where I am and knows where the exit is. It can also be someone who has successfully helped others out of a hole similar to my own. Modern day warrior Kathy Dixon Tondola had the good sense to interview doctors, asking how many patients they had cured of her disorder. And Kathy found her ideal match. (Chapter 17, My Power Tools) Some of my healing partners gave me advice, and others joined me in my situation. Each was good and each contributed to my healing, although working with an ideal partner was the fastest way out.

For almost twenty-five years, I yelled, "Help! Help! I'm in the hole! Please help!" The doctors didn't write a prescription to throw down the hole because they couldn't make a diagnosis. My health declined, and I was frustrated and overwhelmed. I could no longer accept "there are no answers for your conditions, Jane." I was forced to take control if I wanted to recover. It was time to shake things up. I needed a new strategy to find an olympic team of healing partners.

I focused on five points to screen every candidate, and called it "Jane's Olympics Tryout Checklist."

1. Success Rate. Had any of their patients with my symptoms been healed?
2. Attention. Was the practitioner listening to me?
3. Education. Did the practitioner take the time to answer my questions?
4. Team Player. Did the practitioner support my use of alternative treatments?
5. Decision Time. What is my gut telling me to do?

Based on the answers I received, I formed my all-star team of "Jane's Olympians," doctors and other wellness practitioners to lead me out of the hole. I initially relied on them to help me with my physical ailments. Over time, I came to appreciate how they also gave me hope. Jane's Olympians provided support, treatment options, and referrals, and were a mirror to my progress. They inspired my courage and determination to heal.

Jane's Olympians come and go based on my needs and progress. I rely on my checklist to add partners, but I also need to know when to let go. Not everyone gets a long-term contract. When I feel better and get a knowing that it is time to move on, I listen. When I said good-bye to Jill, my rolfer, I had tears in my eyes.

My olympic healing team is made up of not only star practitioners, but also family, friends, and co-workers; priests and other spiritual leaders; and of course, Heavenly Team Jane. Anyone or anything (such as a prayer, nature, an animal, or a pharmaceutical prescription) that helps me reach my wellness goal is a potential member.

I coach an ever-changing relay team of committed healing partners. Reassessing and adjusting the members is now a constant in my life. Jane's Olympians serve as the connective tissue, the fascia, supporting my wellness goals. My health has improved, and I feel stronger and happier. We are aiming for the gold medal.

11

Creating My Unique Healing Formula

"Freedom!"

I had never really thought about my being unique. I focused on the opposite—being like everyone else. For thirty years, I gulped down remedies working for others expecting they'd work for me, too. My focus, drive, and tenacity became detriments when I did not pause to use my common sense and intuition. The price I paid? My pain increased, and I got sicker. Finally I admitted, "Jane, this is not working." Angel messages received. I learned the hard way that blindly following in someone else's footsteps is not the right path for me. I believe we are just like pristine snowflakes that fall in my hometown of Chicago: unique. A customized solution was required for unique Jane.

"Truth is one, paths are many," said Mahatma Gandhi. We may have common symptoms, but I needed to take my own path. My soul yelled, "Freedom!" like Mel Gibson as William Wallace in the movie *Braveheart*. A unique healing formula, as I call my wellness plan, is the mix of healing partners, treatments, and healthy habits from many traditions.

To create my plan, I would need to be resourceful and I accepted the challenge as long as I had fun. Like modern day warrior Jane Borden used ingenuity to become more self-sufficient, I became resourceful. (Chapter 28, The Messenger Bag of Happiness) My approach echoed the game of treasure hunt. Just as in my youth, I use clues (angel tracks) as stepping stones to my treasure (good health). The clues I collect along the way are the components of my unique healing formula.

The six game rules to play Jane's Treasure Hunt to Wellness are refinements of what I learned in Scotland.

1. Stay Alert to Angel Tracks.
2. Wait for Clues.
3. Use Disappointments. "Don't go there if you want to save time."
4. Be Ready to Change.
5. Ask the Body. "Do I Feel Better or Worse?"
6. Keep Going until Cured.

I was ready to begin. Just like a scientist developing a new formula, I had trials and errors, made tweaks and adjustments, and sometimes went back to the drawing board to start from scratch—all the while, understanding this was an investment in me of money, education, and time. Creating my customized wellness formula was a process. As I started healing and realizing my game approach was working, it was a rush. As a bonus prize, my passion for adventure deepened.

Intuitively, I viewed my unique healing formula like a favorite recipe, requiring a variety of ingredients to make the delectable dish. Just like the right mix of butter, milk, sugar, and flour needed for a dessert, I needed the right blend. The hunt was on.

If a clue passes my gut test (that is, I don't get a "nope"), then I give it a go. I keep those that make me feel better and eliminate those that don't. After at least six months, I test the "yeps" to see if they are still needed. For example, I had been practicing yoga regularly for over four years when it was interrupted. What a great opportunity to test the need for yoga in my self-healing formula. My symptoms returned. I took this as a sign that yoga belongs in the maintenance part of my formula.

The results of my yeps? Some clues worked immediately; others took time; and a few didn't work at all. I had instant, positive results from the Mickel Therapy, Richway's Amethyst BioMat, organic sulfur, and a homeopathic remedy. Yoga, acupuncture, Casa herbs, and a crystal bed worked over months. I didn't have luck with Chinese herbs, ionic bracelets, and Western medicine—despite their success for others.

The message? Lighten up. I was careful not to fall into the trap of imposing a time limit on when I expected a clue to work. I took Casa herbs for almost three years before I felt the effects. Modern day warrior Frank Baldassare followed a gluten-free diet for ten years without noticeable improvement. How was he able to stay the course without success? Frank said, "I kept doing it without establishing predetermined goals for it to work. Otherwise, I may end up turning away right on the cusp of a miraculous healing." (Chapter 31, The Perfect Storm)

Yes. Healing takes time. My successful unique healing formula took patience and also a shift in perspective and attitude, action by taking responsibility. Giving up on being healed and receiving miracles was unacceptable to me. I refused to live my life without hope. I chose to walk through fears and evolve into Jane the Explorer. Changing my life was hard work. But the hard work works. My pot of gold? Anything is possible. And I'm never too old to go on another treasure hunt.

PART III.

Jane the Inspirer
(2013–)

I am a work-in-progress. In fact, I have returned to being Jane the Apprentice. Instead of teaching me the tools to self-heal, this time, Heavenly Team Jane is grooming me to sing my soul as Jane the Inspirer. Further, my team is teaching me to serenade the world at a higher octave as a master singer. I'm being inspired to learn how to heal myself with fewer human healing partners, sustain my joy, and evolve into a happy healed healer—as Jane the Inspirer. I am in the midst of this transition, as I recount in the next three chapters.

My first steps as an inspirer intern were to write *You Heal You* and sponsor storytelling events. I continue to look for additional ways to expand the you heal you circle and motivate others to take an active part in their wellness. I may not know where this latest journey will ultimately take me, but I do know the next three steps: me healing me, singing my joy, and becoming a happy healed healer.

Me Healing Me. I had a flashback to Scotland, when, by chance, I healed myself with only Heavenly Team Jane. (Chapter 12, The Wings of a Prayer)

Singing My Joy. Discovering my authentic self gave me the confidence to share my miracles and my personal story. (Chapter 13, The Lightning Rod)

Becoming a Happy Healed Healer. I was given a special invitation to play treasure hunt again. The pot of gold was my second chance in life. (Chapter 14, Next Stop)

Please join me on my newest adventure as I train for Jane the Inspirer. I want to fill—and more importantly, to share—the stage with a growing cast of singers in the you heal you opera.

12

Me Healing Me
The Wings of a Prayer

Nine years ago, I was in Edinburgh and decided to climb Arthur's Seat, a large hill near the center of town. I followed everyone else on the rocky path to the top. While walking around the stony crest, I twisted my old, injured right ankle and had to sit down. I couldn't put any weight on my foot. I panicked. I was alone in a foreign country on top of a large hill, and I couldn't walk. What was I going to do? What is the Scottish equivalent of the United States' 9-1-1? How would I dial it? Would they have to send a helicopter? How else would they get me down the rocky path I had climbed up? Then I got an idea. "Pray, Jane. Just pray." The outcome? My ankle spontaneously healed. I got a glimpse of the possibility of healing myself without an emergency medical team and any other human healing partners. It was the ultimate proof of me healing me.

With much intent and desperation, I prayed to Heavenly Team Jane and any other angels roaming nearby. Then, I got another notion: "Jane, place your hands around your ankle." With everything I had, I envisioned energy going into it. After a while, I let go of my ankle and slowly and carefully stood up. I was able to put pressure on it. I not only walked down Arthur's Seat, but also walked the mile or so back to my hotel. It was a miracle to me. I attributed it to the special energy of a sacred place, rather than a self-activated healing and the power of intent.

As I walked away, I noticed a field of grass slanting to the road on the far side of the mountain. The soft, smooth field provided an easy walk to the road below. An aha moment. By assuming the rest of my walk would be like the beginning—rocky and perilous, I had made my situation worse. The adventure symbolized my healing path to date—bumpy—and my expectation that the rest of my life would be the same.

How many other things in my life was I making harder because of my limited, faulty perception? The following story explains why there are times only I can heal myself, especially in the face of increased difficulty.

A little boy found a caterpillar and brought it home. Every day, he would feed the caterpillar. One day, his new friend started forming a cocoon, and his mother explained how it was transforming into a beautiful butterfly. The little boy watched every day for a butterfly to emerge from its cocoon. At last, he saw part of the butterfly. He watched how hard it struggled to get out, and wanting to help, the little boy slit open its shell. Promptly and easily, the butterfly emerged. But the butterfly couldn't fly, because it still had liquid on its wings. The little boy didn't understand that the struggle through the cocoon would push the liquid from the butterfly's body enabling its wings. The butterfly needed the struggle to fly. As the struggle was avoided, the butterfly could not fly. (Author unknown.)

Struggling through the cocoon prepares a butterfly for independence. Similar to a butterfly, some things in life, I have to do myself. Thank goodness, people in my life (like the little boy) love and care for me, but their efforts may unintentionally slow my recovery if I don't do my part. Through my effort and struggle, I could spread my wings, transform, and soar.

During my healing process, when I completely relied on others and followed their recommendations with little thought and input, I was left wingless and crippled. By letting others slit open my cocoon, I was not doing my part. I had to take control by remaining in the pilot's seat, using my intuition and experience to choose among treatments and healing partners, and deciding when to change both.

I believe each of us has the innate ability to heal ourselves. I am inspired by Frank Salvatore, M.D., as quoted in Emma Bragdon's book *Spiritual Alliances: Discovering the Roots of Health at the Casa de Dom Inácio* (2002).

> *"Sometimes our indoctrinated beliefs get in the way. We have come to believe that patients can not [sic] get well unless they have surgery or drugs, but, sometimes patients can heal themselves without medical intervention from conventional medicine. Where a patient places his or her faith is a potent indicator for healing. Spontaneous remissions do happen. Spiritist healing alone can cure. Prayer can hasten healing."*
> *(Salvatore in Bragdon, I and II)*

I place myself in God's hands. I believe that the cleaner my mind, body, and spirit, the easier my heavenly helpers will move miraculous energy through me. Similar to a car on a free moving interstate, self-maintenance clears my roadblocks just like street cleaning and road repairs. I continually remove poisonous, emotional obstacles and unproductive thoughts (such as anger and self-doubt), destructive substances (foods that my body rejects), and spiritual drains (a faulty belief system and an absence of joy). All obstruct my body's highway and can block my road to God. I work through my layers of grime and remove any new dirt that I accumulate during the day. Cleaning my vessel is a staple in my unique healing formula.

David Mickel, the Scottish medical doctor, was part of my road crew. Eight years ago, he gave me three daily tools to help clear my path. I lovingly disallow unfair treatment; I communicate my feelings honestly; and I meet my needs first. I quickly saw amazing results, especially with my chronic fatigue symptoms.

Believing I could heal myself and then taking control of the process was thrilling. I felt empowered by the satisfaction of a job well done. I began to belly laugh again with my sister Susie. I was moved to write

You Heal You to inspire others to rescue themselves so they, too, can live a more joyful life. Thank you, Heavenly Team Jane, for not giving up on me. You kept at me until I got the message: "All is not lost. Take responsibility. Do for you what needs to be done. It's never too late."

I am still Heavenly Team Jane's you heal you student. Currently, I am working on repeating my miraculous healing similar to the one I had on Arthur's Seat in Edinburgh. Modern day warrior Fotoula Adrimi, who spontaneously aborted her allergic reaction to an insect bite, is my role model. (Chapter 22, My Life Is More Than Stones and Mortar) Although I initially relied heavily on healing partners and their tools, I became more adept at shouldering the responsibility. I took ownership of the tools and was more equipped to heal with less earthly assistance. I have added my belief in self-cure to my unique healing formula.

I now realize the perfection of how my butterfly struggle unfolded. Had I noticed the grassy path before I prayed, I might have tried to shimmy down to the road with a damaged right ankle. Instead, not knowing prompted my first miraculous self-healing. This set the foundation of my belief. The impossible could be possible. Me heal me. You heal you. Let's spread our wings.

13

Singing My Joy
The Lightning Rod

In my family, I was the black sheep wearing a lightning rod on her head, symbolic of my attracting many of the woes. I am eternally grateful for this status, as well as not being spontaneously healed when I first visited Casa de Dom Inacio de Loyola spiritual center in 2009. Both ultimately brought more joy.

A friend told me, "The black sheep is where you want to be, Jane. It has exclusive benefits." Being different forced me to embrace the authentic Jane if I wanted to be happy. Further, I learned I could thrive while marching to the beat of my own drum. I processed things differently than my three siblings. Growing up, I was the one most often sent to her bedroom for misbehaving. In college, I chose the essay question none of my friends did (the easiest to me was the hardest for them). Yep, I was different. And being different set me free.

In addition to being a mischievous child and an atypical test taker, I was the lightning rod of the family. If something deemed unfortunate was going to happen, it probably would happen to me. If someone was going to be laid off from her job, it would be me. If someone was going to remain unmarried, it would be me. If someone was going to break a bone, it would be me. If someone's car was going to hit a deer, it would be mine. If someone's car was to catch on fire, it would be mine. If someone was going to have a head-on collision totaling both cars, it would be me. If someone was going to be diagnosed with mysterious illnesses, of course, it would be me.

My friend was right. Being different has its advantages. And being the lightning rod carries a bonus. As they say, "What doesn't kill you makes you stronger." It certainly did for me. I gained confidence that I could survive life's knocks. After experiencing my top fears, I not only survived but also flourished. My fears now have less hold over me. Attagirl, the worse for wear, warrior Jane.

I dubbed the early years my Calamity Jane stage, but it was really my Lucky Jane phase. Heavenly Team Jane was there all along protecting me and softening the blows. Things could have been so much worse—not to mention, inconvenient. When I broke my ankle, it happened before, not during, a vacation. When my car hit a deer, a local farmer ingeniously duct taped my car so I could drive. When my car caught fire on a country road, I was only a few miles from my parents' house. Heavenly Team Jane stepped in every time.

During my health crisis, I was forced to choose. "Jane, forge your own path or live in pain." Little did I know, marching to the beat of my own drum would help me recover. I was accustomed to doing things my own way. Creating my unique healing formula is just an extension of what I had been doing. Finally, I saw the benefits of being the different one.

And, of course, my undiagnosed illnesses were the best thing that ever happened to me. They changed me to a wounded warrior with a medal of courage. I became adept at dealing with obstacles and seeing the good, and knowing my life would improve because of them. I am no longer so easily intimidated into following the crowd. Been there, done that. And it doesn't work for me. It is easier to follow my passions and be authentic. I started laughing again, and it is from a deeper place. I sing my joy for me being me.

I am also grateful that I was not immediately healed during my first trip to Brazil. Else, I would have continued my life's status quo and missed the thrills as Jane the Explorer and now, as Jane the Inspirer. I wouldn't have met so many remarkable people willing to share their health journeys. I wouldn't be as passionate about self-healing and inspiring others to do the same. I wouldn't have built as intimate a relationship with Heavenly Team Jane, or learned that some of my biggest disappointments are my biggest gifts. I would have remained the same old Jane without any pain.

In Brazil in 2009, God blessed me with something else, something more valuable than a spontaneous healing: the spark of hope. The hope I can sing my joy, regardless of what happens in my life. Just like modern day warrior K. B., who endured rape, substance abuse, and divorce; and she still finds joy in life. (Chapter 25, Just Be) I left that trip more hopeful and much happier than when I had arrived.

The first step for making happiness my life path was to celebrate my uniqueness. More recently, I have discovered that giving to others is my ultimate path to happiness. I can be generous materially (with money), emotionally (with inspirational words), and spiritually (through my thoughts and actions).

I maintain my song of joy through hugs and laughter, and by following my passions. I show my gratitude by giving, and I keep hope in my heart. If you see a sheep with a faded lightning rod on her head hitting the high notes of Gloria Gaynor's "I Will Survive," odds are it's me. Please wave, and I'll wave back.

14

Becoming a Happy Healed Healer
Next Stop

Belief became the foundation of my search for and efforts towards my return to health. I needed to believe anything was possible. Believe I had chosen this life experience for good reasons. Believe my efforts would be worth the investment in myself. Believe life really is a treasure hunt where you search for the good in everything that happens to you. The ups. The downs. The victories. The challenges. It is all perfect. Now, I need to believe I can become a happy healed healer, a master inspirer.

The pot of gold at the end of my treasure hunt initially was good health, but now it is to maintain joy in life. I call those people who have played this game successfully "happy healed healers." They have healed themselves and encourage others to do the same. I am inspired by how modern day warrior Sheri Lynn, after surviving a mother's nightmare, began helping others improve their lives. (Chapter 23, I Have Been to Hell and Learned to Thrive) I, too, intend to play this second-chance-in-life game.

You can usually tell happy healed healers by their actions. They focus on the purpose of their life, love to give, and look for ways to be of service. Although they may not be professional healers, they are passionate about helping others heal. One way they do so is by sharing the stories of their personal experiences—how they naturally sing their soul's joy.

This doesn't mean happy healed healers are joyful 24/7, or that they do not face struggles. Instead, they are distinguished by how they respond. They are grateful for their experiences—physically, emotionally, and spiritually—and step softly and gracefully on their stairway to joy. They are authentic inspirers by walking their talk. Just being around a happy healed healer makes me feel good.

If I hadn't had my seemingly insurmountable challenges, I might not have known about this game of life and met happy healed healers. Lucky Jane. I view those of us with chronic difficulties as the fortunate ones, because we are given a special invitation to play life's treasure hunt. We have the opportunity to make changes and transform. It is never too late. I am singing as I rescue myself along to my next stop: Jane the Inspirer.

PART IV.

Stories of Other Modern Day Warriors

15

P. J. D.

Jiminy Cricket

My name is P. I'm a liar, a cheat, and a thief. I'm self-centered, a pervert, and insane. I am suicidal, bipolar, manic, depressed, alcohol dependent, and capable of doing outrageous things—when I drink. I drink because I have a disease. The disease is alcoholism, a chronic, mental and physical, fatal disease. I was hospitalized for my disease ten times, many of which were lockdowns in mental wards. My prognosis by the doctor, an expert in alcohol dependency, was "grave." I suffered from severe hallucinations and seizures. As my alcohol consumption increased, I lost control of my bladder and bowel function and bled from my rectum daily. My liver was on the verge of not working. My kidneys were weak. My blood pressure alternated between dangerously high and dangerously low.

My weight plummeted from about 210 to 156. My loving wife would make me food, always asking what I wanted. I would force myself to try to eat, but I just couldn't. After a bite or two, I would throw up—sometimes with blood. This became my normal daily ritual. I would then throw the food down the toilet, so she would think I had eaten her carefully prepared meals. One week, I ate only a hard-cooked egg on Wednesday.

At that time, I would also consume at least 1.75 liters of cheap whiskey every day. I shopped at different liquor stores, drank at different bars, and was downing bottles of NyQuil (which contained alcohol) just to help me sleep. I hid the bottles from my wife of forty years so as not to appear to have the problem that was killing me. I had been drinking for almost fifty years and was then sixty. I was physically compelled to drink. I couldn't not drink. I had put myself completely out of my own mind. I became a blackout drinker, not knowing where I was, who I was with, what I was saying, and what I was doing and may have done. I could do things like hurt people and never know it. I remembered nothing. As a child, I liked to finish my parents' drinks. The morning after their parties was always fun. By tenth grade, I was already drinking alcoholically, meaning once I started, I wouldn't stop til I felt the effect. I would drink until drunk––but not every day. My problem wasn't my drinking; my problem was my thinking.

I believed my dad when he told me that I would never amount to anything because I didn't finish what I started. He was trying to make me determined to succeed, but it had the opposite effect. I felt unworthy of any success. I had severe allergies as a kid, and my body was covered in rashes. I was bullied in school and called "Disease" in gym and in pool classes. Back then, the boys swam naked, which didn't help. I was self-conscious about everything. I was pushed around, and so I bullied others to prevent myself from being bullied. But, and here is perhaps the beginning of the miracle inside me, I cried. I cried and I prayed for the other kids who were bullied more than I was. I tried to befriend kids who were bullied when the other bullies weren't around. Then I felt guilty about bullying them in front of the bullies. My self-esteem headed south.

Even as an adult, I tried to be like everyone else—to talk and dress like others. I hated myself. The drink would take away that feeling. Despite having been told that I would amount to nothing, I became a successful advertising executive and had many people working for me. My commercials ran during the Super Bowl. At the after-parties, I would get quite drunk and brag, but it was just a cover-up for my lack of self-worth. I made far more money than I ever dreamed I would, but I was throwing it all away. I was talented, but sick and getting sicker. During my last mental ward lockdown Christmas 2009, my miracle began to happen. I thought I had God in my life. I prayed to God, who I sometimes referred to as "Jiminy Cricket" since God whispered in my ear as the Walt Disney character did in *Pinocchio*. I knew I was living wrong, but never listened to this voice of conscience that was always there.

Meanwhile, in the hospital, I began to draw with the bits of crayons and any paper left in the patient dining room. I drew my version of "The Twelve Days of Christmas." I always added three crows in the air, which has spiritual significance to me. Other patients began to draw with me. Some of them added the three flying crows to their drawings, but we never talked about why. I helped them learn how to draw. I was a talented artist, but hated everything I drew.

After our meals, I collected the unused cups of Half & Half, milk, syrup, and jelly. Others followed suit. I showed my fellow crazy friends how to make milkshakes. Hey, they would have tossed them out anyway. My friends liked the milkshakes, and I liked thinking of my friends instead of myself. This began to heal me, although I didn't know it at the time.

Since my release from the mental institution, I have learned that when you can put the man next to you or behind you, in front of you, you will know the spirit inside of you—the power I call "God." The spirit greater than you and me who turns on the light in the sky each morning, seeds our food, and cleanses and heals all. God, my Jiminy Cricket, has been and is a loyal friend and my moral conscience. When I realized this, I stopped drinking. From the gates of death—my hell on earth—I arrived at a whole new world that I never imagined was there for me.

About three months later, one morning, I stopped at McDonald's for an Egg McMuffin, hash browns, and a coffee. (Remember the egg I ate that Wednesday and threw up?) On the way to my truck with food in hand, I started to cry out loud. "God, why me? Please help the people who really need it. I'm OK." I felt so good that I wasn't drinking anymore and was actually eating, while so many people struggled.

People who have lost it all. People in jail cells. People far worse off than I was. People I know, such as my new friends from the meetings.

I got into my truck and turned the ignition key. My country music was playin' on m' pick-up truck's FM. It was a beautiful, sunny day. I took a bite of the hash browns. Then holding the rosary that my mom had given me as a kid (it hangs from the mirror), I prayed for those worse off than me. Something strange started to happen. I felt myself leaving myself. I dunno any other way to describe it. I could feel something in me, something rising up from me. I was frightened like never before. I thought I was dying. All of a sudden, I heard (or felt) these words, "Don't worry, P., your job's not done yet." I will never forget it. A feeling of calm and peace came over me like I had never felt before or since. That day, you could have cut off my arm, and I would have thanked you. I felt light—almost high—all day. That moment, I knew I could never drink again. It was a spiritual intervention of sorts. I pray a lot now for others and for the power to help others.

Today, the obsession to drink has left me. Material things once important to me have become meaningless. A chipmunk running across the grass evokes tremendous emotion and gratitude. I say "thank you" now for the littlest thing because no little thing is little. In the shower, I talk to our Creator and thank Him for the waters that bring new life. I ask that those waters cleanse and heal me inside and out. I ask for blessings and healing for those who struggle. What happens to me tomorrow is of little importance to me today. Ten out of every ten people die. When I die and how I die isn't up to me, so it matters not. But my greatest gift—alcoholism—almost did kill me.

December 21, 2009, at my family's intervention, my son, with tears coming down his face, hugged me. "Dad, don't you want to be alive to meet your grandchildren?" Two years later, on my sixty-second birthday, my granddaughter was born. They say she and I share a special bond. Eighteen months later, my grandson was born. I never say that "I've got to" watch my grandchildren; I say, "I get to." I get to do everything I do. Life is a gift, and my gift is every day. Thanks to many doctors of mind and body, clergymen, and spiritual advisors, today, I am well—by the grace of God (Jiminy Cricket). You are the miracle inside me. All I did was make a decision, and go to battle against myself. I pray you, the reader, will find your miracle—in you. Then, you can heal you.

P. J. D. is a retired advertising executive in Buffalo, New York.

16

Yorli Huff

Choose a Positive Outcome

Some people doubt that miracles exist. But I don't. The word "miracle" is certainly no stranger to me. It's more like a childhood friend who occasionally stops by to catch up. Heck, it was even in the room the moment I was born.

As they say down South, I was born "with a veil over my face." The more generally accepted description of my condition is that I was born "with the caul," meaning still in the amniotic sac. As my mother later told me, I was a determined baby, ready to see the light of day. My mother's sudden, powerful contractions prevented her from making it to the hospital. So my grandmother delivered me at home. For this reason, I consider my life a miracle from day one. My grandmother, who had no experience whatsoever in childbirth techniques, delivered a healthy, happy baby girl. My mother told me that I didn't come into this world crying like other babies: I was singing and cooing.

When God decided it was time for me to have a child of my own, I was visited by another miracle. My son was born premature, at twenty-four weeks, and a Code Blue was called. Doctors told me that if my baby boy didn't die, he would be severely retarded. As I looked at this little fighter the size of my hand, I never doubted that he would make it through this without a scratch. When his miniature hand squeezed my pinky, I was certain.

In boot camps and seminars, I mentor teens about our life paths. I often use the analogy of a GPS tracking system. When you get in that car as a teenager, you want to go but you have no idea what address to enter in your navigation machine. It's going to take some work to know where to go, but you have a journey and a path. Every driver has run into some construction or an unexpected accident and is forced to take a minor, brief detour from the main road. Life is full of these surprise re-routes, and I know that just as well as anyone else.

I am a chosen soul with a unique gift and mission, sent here by God to serve. Each morning, I thank God for choosing me. I stand in front of the bathroom mirror and say, "I intend to attract the career I desire into my life. I do what I do because it's my purpose and my destiny. I am debt free. I intend to attract multiple streams of wealth and prosperity in unlimited abundance. I am in divine health. I attract the power to strengthen my immune system, mind, body, and soul."

The beginning of my life was tumultuous. From an early age, I was subjected to molestation by a family member, had low self-esteem, lacked family support, and was often degraded and alienated—despite having an intact and stable family structure. I was raised by my grandparents who were two generations removed from slavery, so a lot of baggage carried into my upbringing spilled over onto me.

As a result of these experiences, I initially had trouble valuing my body, which led to my two teen pregnancies and abortions. I also self-inflicted abuse, refusing to face my problems. I was tested again when my husband, who had once threatened to kill me, decided to take his own life. However, I feel that I am privileged to have experienced all of that because if I hadn't gone through those troubles, I could never be a source of inspiration to others. Enduring my husband's suicide after my early life difficulties gave me a broader understanding of the pain that destroys some people.

In 1994, at age twenty-four, I was the caregiver to my grandparents and in the police academy. I became an undercover agent for the Cook County Sheriff's Police Department in Chicago. I thought I had landed my dream job. Never in my wildest dreams did I imagine that my life would soon start spiraling out of control. I was one of few female agents and even fewer female African-American agents on the task force, and was subjected to sexual and racial discrimination. I became a victim of intimidation and extreme fear tactics. I received death threats, and my house was even set on fire. I decided to take my battle to court, despite being advised that I had no shot in a lawsuit against the Cook County Sheriff's Police Department. When I received the death threats, I stood firm and told my persecutors to bring their whole arsenal and make sure I'm no longer breathing if they ever try to kill me, because I'm ready for battle.

I filed and lost an employment discrimination lawsuit against the Cook County Sheriff's Department, and then I appealed. Jeffrey I. Cummings, my attorney for the appeal, told me that despite the strength of my evidence, the odds were strongly against me. He cited a study of the results of federal appeals between 1988 and 2004 that showed employment discrimination plaintiffs who lost after a federal trial won only 9 percent of their appeals (178 out of 2,042). *See* Clermont, Kevin M. and Schwab, Stewart J., "Employment Discrimination Plaintiffs in Federal Courts: From Bad to Worse?" (2009), *Cornell Law Faculty Publications*, at page 110.

My trial took eleven years to win, but in the end, I had done what everyone said was impossible. The verdict turned out in my favor because I simply chose differently from my doubters. I compare this court case to the birth of my son. Despite my doctor's words, I knew deep in my heart that my son would live to be a healthy boy. Why? Because I chose a happy outcome. And despite the warnings of my friends, family, and legal team, I won my discrimination case. Why? Because I chose to approach every day with a positive outlook and a clenched fist.

All of my experiences in life helped me understand my divine purpose—what God created me to be. Since my birth in the caul, God has been and remains my guide on this journey. He chose me to be a jack-of-all-trades, a knight to accomplish whatever he wants to be done at the time. I know this because so many of my life experiences prepared me perfectly for what would come next. Growing up as the caregiver of my grandmother, I became accustomed to hospitals and learned how to interact with doctors. Those times prepared me for my son's birth. We never stop learning and growing—until we die. Everything in life is an opportunity. When I now choose each event's outcome, my back straightens and my heart lightens.

For many years, I was crippled by anger. During my twenties, I held a lot of frustration inside about my molestation, and when I got angry, I could feel my body temperature rise a few degrees. In my efforts to avoid my conscious thought and to distract myself from my problems, I took on three jobs on top of going to school. I remember watching an episode of *The Oprah Winfrey Show* about forgiveness, and realizing that I had to come to terms with my past. I was so bogged down with spiritual weight that I had knots in my back. By developing better habits, I regained my self-confidence. I learned that when someone hurts you, he isn't thinking about you, but of himself. By holding onto your anger you give the other person your power. This realization was a major breakthrough for me.

Each of us is wondrous and unique, and the world is just waiting for our contribution. God has given each of us a personal lottery ticket. As we grow, we achieve some self-awareness and come to realize that we're here to serve others. When you see your life experiences as a gift and share your gifts with the world, you cash in your personal lottery ticket. The beautiful part is that you'll be rewarded on earth just as much as you will be in heaven.

Yorli Huff is the founder of Engendering Strength Inc., created to encourage others to adopt a different mindset, trust God, and pursue one's victory. In 2010, she published *The Veil of Victory—A Memoir of Triumph and Tragedy*. Yorli lives with her son in Naperville, Illinois. *superherohuff.com*

Jeffrey I. Cummings works as a United States Magistrate Judge in Chicago, where he is responsible for a variety of duties in federal civil and criminal cases. Judge Cummings started his career as a law clerk for a United States District Court Judge and then worked at a law firm where he represented a variety of clients in federal and state civil cases and specialized in representing plaintiffs in cases involving employment discrimination, whistleblower protection, civil rights, and voting rights. Judge Cummings received a BA from Michigan State University with a double major in public policy and graduated with high honors and as a member of Phi Beta Kappa. He then received his JD from Northwestern University School of Law, where he graduated cum laude and as a member of the Order of the Coif. Judge Cummings is married and has a daughter.

17

Kathy Dixon Tondola
My Power Tools

The only reason my story is a miracle is because others are still suffering from this and I am not. My "this" is an anxiety disorder. It started one night when I went to bed and tried to fall asleep. I had been cleaning the house late on a Friday night so I could free up the rest of the weekend. I was tired but at the same time, wound up. It didn't help that a young neighbor was talking to my husband about "stuff." I wasn't comfortable with this man being in our house and felt anxious as I was trying to fall asleep. About thirty minutes later, my heart started beating quickly. I was dizzy, felt like I couldn't breathe, and was paralyzed by fear.

I weakly called out to my husband (now deceased), Darryl, and whispered to him what I was feeling. I added, "If you call an ambulance, I will have a heart attack because the whole scene will be way too stressful." He instructed the young man to go home, and I sat a quarter of the way up—the only way I seemed able to breathe.

For the next five hours, in addition to all of the other symptoms, I experienced waves of fear and dread. Darryl called my sister so she could talk me into going to the hospital. They were both very afraid. She finally convinced me, with the understanding that I would ride in her car.

I went to the emergency room and took many tests, which showed nothing. I was sent home and told to follow up with my doctor, which I did. He said it sounded like a panic attack, but didn't really give me any more help or information. I didn't know what a panic attack was, and this had never happened to me before. I did a little research, but found only a list of symptoms that other sufferers had reported and no explanation of why or what to do.

My panic/anxiety disorder lasted five years. The attacks ranged from one to several a week. They could last several hours, and the symptoms were severe. This was later diagnosed as a panic disorder. I started "treatment" by phone with my mother-in-law, who prayed me through them no matter when they hit. I only called her when they were really bad. (The really bad ones lasted hours.) I would walk back and forth through the house, yelling out scriptures to get rid of the evil spirit that possessed me. My initial symptoms paved the way for other symptoms. During an attack, I was convinced that I was dying. Whenever they ended, I cried with relief.

I was in the emergency room five times and hospitalized (and drugged) in the psychiatric ward for one week. Ironically I had no panic attacks in the ward, because I slept all the time—even through the sessions with the psychiatrists. When I left, I was prescribed Xanax (a drug to treat anxiety and panic disorder) and referred to a psychiatrist. After six months of seeing him and not getting better, I asked him if he had ever cured someone of this. The doctor admitted that I was his first patient with this, and he didn't know too much about it.

I stopped seeing him and asked my primary care doctor to recommend someone who had more experience treating patients with my condition. That is how I came to see Dave C., PhD, in Rolling Meadows, Illinois, and how I was cured of my panic/anxiety disorder.

During the first session, Dr. C. taught me how to breathe by contracting the diaphragm during an attack so that I wouldn't hyperventilate, which worsens the symptoms. He also spun me around in a chair, called "desensitization," to mimic the dizziness I felt during the attacks. Dr. C. pointed out that I did not die from my dizziness or from any other attack I had had. In just one hour with this doctor, I was on my way. The exercises decreased my attacks by 50 percent in one week.

At the second visit, Dr. C. gave me sheets to record the intensity and the symptoms of each attack—a panic diary. This was to be done while I was having an attack. No easy feat, I tell you. Then Dr. C. taught me a song: "I'm gonna have an attack and die, doo-dah, doo-dah." I thought he was nuts, and I was not amused. At that point, it was not funny. I never did sing that song, but I understood the reason. It was another way to desensitize the fear the attacks bring, namely the fear of dying. The second visit decreased my attacks even more.

In the third week's meeting, Dr. C. and I discussed the symptoms and my feelings during the attacks. This decreased my attacks by 90 percent—in three weeks.

I have not had an attack for many years. Thank you, God, and for your miracle in the form of Dr. C., who stopped my attacks by showing me tools to take away their power.

Kathy Dixon Tondola is a compliance supervisor for a major financial and insurance firm in Chicago. For over four decades, she has held various positions in the financial industry. Kathy has two sons and five grandchildren, and volunteers for an organization that helps teen moms. She travels extensively and looks forward to her next season of life.

18

Delizia Cirolli-Costa

A Lourdes Christmas Miracle

May 2015, I traveled to Lourdes, a small town in the foothills of the Pyrenees in southwest France. The Sanctuary of our Lady of the Lourdes, a Catholic pilgrimage site, attracts around three million visitors annually. For five months in 1858, Bernadette Soubirous, a local, fourteen-year-old girl, reported having seen eighteen Apparitions (later revealed to be the Blessed Virgin Mary). Since then, there have been about seven thousand cases of unexplained cures (according to current scientific knowledge) recorded. Having met rigorous standards of review, sixty-nine cases, or one percent, have been deemed miraculous by a bishop of the Catholic Church through 2015. I am impressed by the Catholic Church's thorough investigation of miracle healings, a rigor similar to the canonization process for sainthood. For example, an account is automatically eliminated if there has been any treatment at any time for the condition. The case of Delizia Cirolli-Costa lasted twelve years and became miracle number sixty-five. The story of Delizia Cirolli-Costa is reprinted with permission from the Medical Bureau of Lourdes, whom I interviewed June 4. Certain events and facts, set off in brackets and footnoted, are from additional sources. Date formats, some place names, and spellings have been Americanized. You may read more about this at "The Medical Bureau of the Sanctuary," *the Official Website of the Sanctuary Our Lady of Lourdes (France), lourdes-france.org/en/medical-bureau-sanctuary/.*

—*Jane G. Doyle*

Delizia Cirolli-Costa[1]
Born November 17, 1964
Living in Paternò, Sicily, Italy

Recognized June 28, 1989
by Bishop Luigi Bonmarito

At the beginning of March 1976, the eleven-year-old Delizia Cirolli from Paternò presented the first signs of a seemingly ordinary illness, an inflamed and painful right knee.

After some worrying x-ray results, she was admitted to the University Orthopaedic Clinic where she remained from April 30 until May 17, 1976.

There a surgical biopsy of the topmost extremity of the right tibia [shinbone—Ed.] confirmed the dreaded diagnosis of **a malignant bone tumor**. [Emphasis in original—Ed.]

In view of the seriousness of the illness and the absolutely hopeless prognosis, palliative therapy was recommended (amputation and radiotherapy).

This was refused by [t]he child's parents who preferred to bring her back home to her own milieu, with her family around her.

[Summer 1976, "thanks to the generosity of friends, Delizia made a pilgrimage to Lourdes with her mother. She returned exhausted but without any change, and certainly not cured."[2]]

It was [sic] until Christmas 1976, when her life seemed more and more under threat (she weighed no more than twenty-two kilograms [forty-eight-and-a-half pounds—Ed.], though her local community was praying for her) that suddenly there appeared the first signs of her cure.

---

1. Originally published as "Delizia Cirolli-Costa," in *Cures of Lourdes Recognized as Miraculous by the Church*, Bureau des Constatations Médicales, Sanctuaire Notre-Dame de Lourdes (May 2011). All rights reserved. Reprinted with permission.

2. Théodore Mangiapan, "[case number] 65 / Delizia Cirolli," in *Lourdes: Miraculous Cures—Who, When, and Where!* (Lourdes, France: Imprimerie de la Grotte, 1987), 138.

Very quickly she began to lead a normal life again, to eat once more, to go to school beginning in January, and to grow and develop.

In July 1977, she returned to Lourdes with her mother who was eager to make known this cure to the doctors of the Medical Bureau [of Lourdes, the department charged with investigating medical miracle claims—Ed.] and so, for the first time (in Lourdes) the child was examined and her medical records assessed.

From a clinical point of view all that remained was a significant residual deformity of the axis of the lower limb "in genu valgum" [knock-knee—Ed.]. Two sets of x-rays showed a very satisfactory development of the front bone lesion, a development that was totally unexpected.

Consequently Delizia presented herself at the Medical Bureau, so that her cure could be checked, in July 1978 and 1979 during a U.N.I.T.A.L.S.I. [Unione Nazionale Italiana Trasporto Ammalati a Lourdes e Santuari Internazionali—Ed.] pilgrimage from eastern Sicily. Each time she was examined by several doctors and found to be in perfect health, growing and developing at a normal rate for her age.

On July 28, 1980, she was examined again and several checks were carried out. There was nothing specific left apart from the persistence of the "genu valgum," a correction of which was considered for the coming year.

Nearly four years had passed since the cure [sic] the original and malignant tumor (the diagnosis and prognosis of which were in no doubt) with no specific treatment that would favor or explain this return to a normal condition, and despite the evident after-effect (the deformity of the lower right member), a clear sign of the lesional character of the illness.

That day the Medical Bureau of Lourdes decided, by a majority of members present, to consider the cure "given the conditions in which it was effected and maintained as a phenomenon contrary to the observations and predictions of medical experience, and scientifically inexplicable." The case was submitted to the International Medical Committee of Lourdes [C.M.I.L.—Ed.] for its assessment and consideration. At its meeting of September 26, 1982[,] this court of second instance for checking miracles at Lourdes studied:

- The opinion of the Diocesan Medical Commission made up of doctors and surgeons involved in treating the patient
- The medical report drawn up by Professor A. Trifaud of France and B. Colvin of Scotland.

After a thorough discussion of these[,] the C.M.I.L. considered—almost unanimously—that the cure, in the absence of any treatment and verified after a period of six years, of the malignant growth of the upper extremity of the right tibia suffered by Delizia Cirolli, constituted a quite exceptional phenomen[on], in the strictest sense of the term, contrary to all observation and prediction known to medical experience and, moreover, was inexplicable.

The patient and meticulous canonical investigation ended on June 28, 1989, Msgr. Luigi Bonmarito, Archbishop of Catania, solemnly recognized the miraculous character of this cure and its value as a "sign." He encouraged the faithful "to give thanks for this gift from God to his Church[,]" which, he stated, "had been obtained through the intercession of the Blessed Virgin" in response to men's heartfelt prayers.

Meanwhile, Delizia, as she had hoped, had had surgery on the residual "genu valgum" in 1988. She had got[ten] married two years previously, having obtained in 1985 her state nursing diploma. Very faithfully she comes to Lourdes with the sick pilgrims by train and very discre[e]tly— witnesses to the grace she has received.

19

L. A.

My Mother Would Not Have Recognized Me

I suffered with arthritis for thirty years. Then one day during my Yi Ren Qigong (pron. YEE-ren CHEE-gung) exercises, an energy medicine practice, I had a spontaneous healing. I thought I had conquered my most serious health issue. Well, I was wrong. Four months after my healing from arthritis, I learned that I had lupus. My body could no longer differentiate between healthy tissue and a foreign invader, and began to wage war against the good guys. The autoimmune disease is incurable and chronic.

One day after practicing yoga on my deck, I rested on the mat to integrate the exercises into my body and experienced a beam of light penetrating the corner of my left eye. Within fifteen minutes, my left eye began to swell. Odd but not a big deal, so I ignored it. Several days later, both eyes were swollen and a reddish patch appeared around my eyes and cheeks. I assumed my mild seasonal allergies were recurring, but more severely this spring. And so, I went to the doctor for allergy relief. But each day, I got a little worse. Some periods of the day, my eyes would swell shut. After a couple of weeks, I had lost ten pounds. I had no appetite, a constant sore throat, maintained a low-grade fever, was completely exhausted, and wore glasses to protect my eyes from glare.

One evening, my face swelled uncontrollably. Four antihistamines brought no relief, and I was getting much worse. My face was about thrice its normal size, and my eyes were swollen shut. My best friend, Wendy, decided to surprise me with take-out Chinese food and was knocking on the door. When I opened the door, she took one look at me and said, "Get in the car. Now!" We rushed to the ER.

The triage nurse admitted me immediately. I decided I was fine and really did not want to be at the hospital, so I stood and walked toward the door. On my way to the exit, I passed a mirror and happened to glance at my reflection. I was stunned. I did not recognize myself. My mother would not have recognized me. I consented to treatment and followed the nurse and Wendy to the doctor's examination room.

The doctor came in, saw me, and instantly said, "You do not have allergies; you have lupus." I had no idea what lupus was and knew nothing about the condition. I was given steroids and a heavy-duty antihistamine. Wendy helped me with the medication until I was aware enough to remember to take it. Thank goodness for angels, such as Wendy.

Still swollen and tremendously fatigued and groggy from the prescribed medications, I recuperated at home for three weeks. Remarkable experiences transpired. One evening, I thought the word "harmony," and a jolt of energy shot up my leg from my big toe to my torso. Shocked, I repeat the word, and the jolt recurred. This went on several more times with the same energetic response. I learned later that energy was shooting up the pancreas meridian. (The meridians are internal pathways or energy channels running throughout the body.) We talk about energy being subtle, but this was not subtle. It was shockingly strong.

Later that evening, seated at the table to eat, I brought the fork to my mouth and felt a sharp, stabbing pain in my shoulder blade, which is associated with the small intestine energy pathway. Each time I brought the fork to my mouth, I felt the pain. They were correlated somehow. Yikes.

I got up and took food out of the cupboards and lined up the twenty-five to thirty boxes and cans and bottles along the counter. Standing in front of each item for several minutes, I observed my shoulder blade before moving onto the next item. The foods that caused the pain now and when I ate were foods I was not supposed to eat. For instance, grains are known to be pro-inflammatory, and I found all grains to be unacceptable.

I had experienced shoulder pain for several months whenever I sat in front of a computer. I thought I had pulled a muscle, but instead, my body was sending me a message. It was telling me that the activity was not healthy (just like the food that caused the pain was not healthy).

Usually with our diets, we eat and then have a bad reaction if it's not the best for our system, but my body was warning me before I ate. I had a built-in 24/7 alert system monitoring my exposures to unhealthy food, electronics, places, people, and thoughts. I was amazed.

The next day, I felt an intense buzzing at the index knuckle of my right hand and when I pressed it, the shoulder pain stopped. I could neutralize external disturbances, such as food allergies, by pressing the point on my knuckle. I learned that the index finger is associated with the large intestine energy pathway. By pressing the point on my hand, I stimulated the large intestine meridian. I activated its function at the energy level and released the shoulder pain located in the small intestine meridian.

Not only did my body send me a warning signal about the physical stimuli, but also I soon learned that it alerted me to negative thoughts. Each time my thoughts were negative, nasty, fearful, or unhealthy, I got zapped. My body was training me to eliminate negativity and to make healthy choices instead of my patterned, unhealthy choices. Before the zap, I had no idea that the choices I was making were not the best for me.

At first I thought this system was great, until I got zapped constantly because a lot of organic and fresh food I was eating was not the best for me. I became annoyed and testy. I didn't want to give up some of my bad habits. Then I realized how life-giving and supportive my alert system was, and I came to honor my body. That was the day I let go of my anger and thanked my body. Over time, I adopted better habits and no longer got zapped continually.

Then the intense electrical vibration or buzzing sensation traveled deeper into my shoulder blade along the Chong Meridian, which is associated with the endocrine system. I learned about myself, about what my body needed or didn't need. My body's reliable alert mechanism guided my choices without delusion, excuses, and intellectual reason. My body never lied regarding what was a good or bad choice—either strengthening or hindering my immune system. The system connects my conscious mind. And I noted my many negative thoughts.

Four months before my diagnosis, in 2005, I had begun studying Yi Ren Qigong to be able to help people confined to hospital beds or wheelchairs learn to move gently. Street clothes are worn, and no special shoes, attire, and equipment are required.

The ancient science of Qigong and its exercises stimulate and channel the body's Qi-energy and life force towards nourishment and healing. My Qigong teacher Dr. Guan-Cheng Sun founded the Institute of Qigong & Integrative Medicine (IQ&IM) in 1997, in Bothell, Washington. He treats patients for chronic fatigue, sleep disorders, weight loss, and other health concerns.

Shortly after my diagnosis, in one of the seminars I often attended, Dr. Sun discussed how every illness has its own particular consciousness. I asked about lupus, and he said the internal consciousness was dominated by blame and guilt, emotions associated with the pancreas. Pieces of the puzzle were coming together. The energy shooting up from my big toe to my torso went to my pancreas to release excess accumulations of blame and guilt. It was then that I started to heal.

Dr. Sun added that I could be taking on other people's blame and guilt. Although not my own, if allowed to accumulate without awareness, my body would perceive the negativity as its own. This could lead to self-blame and guilt, which can result in self-punishment and self-attack. When the immune system received the signals of self-sabotage, symptoms of lupus could easily occur. To change the internal consciousness, Dr. Sun suggested that I build up kidney energy, harmonize the pancreas and stomach, release liver accumulation, and energize the small intestine/heart energy to bring self-love and self-nourishment energy.

I had a healing session with Dr. Sun, practiced specific Yi Ren Qigong exercises daily, changed my diet, and found the most nourishing actions in every area of my life. Within nine months, I felt great. After my spontaneous healing from arthritis and the body communications from my lupus, I began investigating the body's Qi-energy communications because it had ignited the process of my awareness and change.

L. A. has an extensive background in Qigong, dance, yoga, Pilates, and herbal medicine.

Dr. Guan-Cheng Sun is the founder and executive director of the Institute of Qigong & Integrative Medicine (IQ&IM) in Bothell, Washington, and a research scientist and adjunct faculty member at Bastyr University in Kenmore, Washington. Dr. Sun earned his PhD in molecular genetics from the Graduate University for Advanced Studies in Japan in 1993. Dr. Sun developed and refined an integrated system of Qigong exercises to activate and cultivate the body's authentic Qi-energy, life force, and intelligence for self-healing, self-care, and self-fulfillment. Yi Ren Qigong is an ancient classics-based, outcome-based, science-based, and evidence-based innovative energy medicine modality. Dr. Sun offered the first medical Qigong education program at a university for health-care professionals. He is also an expert in self-healing and self-care protocols for Type 2 diabetes, chronic pain, cancer prevention, chronic fatigue, insomnia, weight loss, and other health concerns.
iqim.org

20

Catherine Kominos
Cracking the Safe to My Heart

My heart was being shuttered behind steel doors, as if sealed inside a dark vault. Like a faintly imaged movie projected on a small screen, I saw it happening. It felt like a dream, but I was awake. In 1968, I was an eight-year-old, new emigrant from Greece. Shy and introverted, I was ostracized at school in Washington, D.C. Girls can be mean, and I felt profoundly rejected. To protect it from future hurts, my heart remained locked away for the next three-plus decades.

My need to belong drove me to succeed academically and professionally. I stayed in Washington, studied engineering, became a design engineer, and worked at the Pentagon. I relished working in a man's world. At twenty-five, I married Sassan Babaie, an Iranian-born telecom executive. We had two children. My parents lived nearby. Life was busy and full, but comfortable for many years.

January 1, 2000, Sassan and I celebrated the New Millennium at home and then went to sleep. I was woken by a loud voice: "Something bad will happen to Sassan." Assuming I had been dreaming, I ignored the voice and went back to sleep. Then I heard the voice again, "Something bad will happen to Sassan." This time I got scared, but still said nothing to my husband fast asleep by my side.

In the morning I called my mother, who interprets dreams, and asked her if the voice I had heard was a warning. She had just cut the vasilopita (king pie), containing a hidden coin said to bear good luck to the receiver, to welcome the new year as is the Greek custom. Sassan's slice contained the coin. "He'll be lucky this year, Rina," my mother assured me.

On Valentine's Day, Sassan complained of double vision. Two weeks later, he was hospitalized. Lymphoma (a cancer of the blood) was suspected, but March 10, we received far more dire news. My young husband had stage IV glioblastoma multiforme, the most aggressive form of primary brain tumor. The usual prognosis is three months. I talked to every research hospital, and there was nothing more they could do. I was in shock.

Leaving the hospital each night to go home to our kids, I would drive by St. Catherine of Siena Catholic Church in Great Falls, Virginia. One evening as I passed, I again heard the loud voice from New Year's: "Come inside." So I did. My eyes fell on a painting of the Virgin Mary. I stared into her eyes and was pulled into another realm. I had never before experienced such a state of peace—absolute stillness that caused every inch of my body to fully relax, my thoughts to cease, and the emotional storm raging within me to quiet. It felt like an embrace from the Divine.

On the worst day of my life, when the oncologist told me that Sassan had at most three months remaining, the Divine made its presence felt. This first spiritual experience continued to carry an intensity that eventually impacted my consciousness. The state of absolute peace lingered and helped me remain calm and strong and purposeful as I ordered the crumbled pieces of my shattered life.

Days later, a Pentagon coworker asked me, "How open are you? My wife has a friend who's a healer. She's healed people of cancer. She's been touched by the Blessed Mother" (the Virgin Mother). The latter again resonated with me; I am Greek Orthodox, although non-practicing. I called Kenna S., and she became Sassan's healer and later my teacher. She trained with Barbara Brennan, author of *Hands of Light*. Kenna started to work on Sassan remotely, who was also receiving radiation and chemotherapy. I trusted Kenna, even if I didn't understand what she was doing. She sometimes asked me to lift up Sassan from his hospital bed to strengthen his muscles as she worked on different areas of his body, which was paralyzed from the neck down.

And then, a miracle happened. April 13, to the astonishment of the oncologist and neurologist, Sassan walked out of the hospital. I turned to spirituality as a mission and took it on as aggressively as I do any project—with purpose. I threw myself in and pushed with impatience. By grace, the universe guided me to spiritual masters, modern day saints, and powerful healers, and on pilgrimages and other experiences. I was able to let go of my anger and resentment and accept my life.

In October, my husband and I made a pilgrimage to Lourdes, France, and while there, I experienced the inflow of cosmic energy as a powerful vibratory sensation throughout my body. It felt as if a fire hydrant opened up at the top of my head and the energy gushed through me with such force that I could not move, and was then replaced by intense heat. My body felt as if roasted from the inside out. I tried to cry out for help, but no words came. I later learned that it was a healing, a spiritual baptism of the Holy Spirit with fire, as described in the Bible.

Seven months later, May 2001, Sassan's brain tumor was gone, and we planned a second pilgrimage—this time, to Israel and Mount Tabor (the site of the Transfiguration of Jesus, according to Christian belief).

Upon our return home from Israel, the tumor came back. Sassan was dying, and I was beyond myself in grief, fear, pain, and hopelessness. I began to have repeated visions of Mother Mary and of Jesus Christ. I felt their loving essence permeate my home. Again in my darkest hours, I was supported by the loving comfort of God. During my daily meditative walk through the wooded trails along the Potomac River, I asked God, "Why are you putting me through this? Why are you allowing Sassan to die?" Other times, I exploded in pain and rage. I screamed to the trees about the injustice of it all.

Then, September 21, 2001, what felt like a nuclear explosion went off in my heart. Sassan, age forty-two, died. I held his hand as he took his last breath. I stepped away from my husband's cold body, went outdoors, lit a cigarette, and stared at the stars.

The next years were increasingly difficult. I was angry and resentful. Life felt like a living hell. One desperate evening, I cried out, "I'm done." Jesus Christ appeared in a vision, "Do you choose life?" And I did, because of my kids. Life was still tumultuous but ultimately healing.

I immersed myself in spirituality. The esoteric practices of Sufism, alchemy, Christian mysticism, and Kundalini yoga helped tap my well of grief. From the teachings of the Sufi mystic Pir Vilayat Inayat Khan, I learned the art of self-observation. I studied the use of sacred geometries to alchemically transform limiting beliefs and negative emotions. On the island of Cyprus, studying with Panayiota, a Christian mystic, I learned to work with my etheric body to travel among space, time, and dimensions. The etheric body (also known as the "light body" or "subtle body") is the first layer in the human energy field (the "aura").

As life continued to throw obstacles on my path, I used the spiritual tools learned in the various mystical traditions to gently leap over the hurdles and keep going. I became certified to teach Kundalini yoga in 2005 and attended numerous yoga retreats in Española, New Mexico. The retreats were transformative. As fifteen hundred or so yogis chanted in unison under the large pavilion, I was able to cry out my grief undisturbed and release more of my emotional pain. Finally, I felt cleansed and purified of the burden of carrying heavy suitcases filled with my sorrow. I was free.

Through numerous spiritual practices, such as breathing love into the heart, polishing the heart (by constantly clearing out negative emotions), intensive breathwork (pranayama), and guided meditations, my heart began to reawaken. At first, my heart hurt as if I was having a heart attack, but the doctor confirmed nothing was physically wrong with me. The heart pain was from stretching open what had been closed. As self-limiting beliefs peeled away, my light expanded. People said I looked radiant and asked for my beauty secret. I said, "I have undergone an alchemical transformation from being a lump of coal into gold."

But the path wasn't smooth. As I neared each breakthrough, doubts would arise. My yoga teacher said the personality reacts to the threat of annihilation with resistance. I pushed through it by establishing a daily spiritual practice. I would rise at 4:30 a.m. to do yoga postures, meditate, chant, and read scripture.

Then one morning, I realized my anger and resentment arose because I felt alone, having been betrayed and abandoned. Yet God had other plans for me, plans that necessitated an open and loving—not a sealed—heart. So as life progressed, I was tested over and over on these two issues.

Pilgrimages to sacred sites with Earth-Keeper were another avenue of spiritual growth. During travels in the United States, Bolivia, and Egypt, I have had past-life visions of traumas I carried over many life-times. In 2013, I took a sacred journey back to Greece. I connected with the Muses at Delphi and had a profound experience with Mother Mary at a remote monastery on the island of Patmos, where Saint John received the Book of Revelations.

Each struggle could be viewed as an instrument in the drama of my life, bringing up stuff that had to be cleared. Each played a role in the evolution of my soul. I had been too comfortable to change anything about my life with Sassan to be able to heal. My entire journey was the opening of my heart to love.

Did I crack the safe? Did the screws unbolt? Midway through my spiritual awakening and healing trainings, I practiced yoga/Qigong (pron. CHEE-gung) with teacher George McFadden. We met twice weekly at 6 a.m. for a year. We had just completed many intense Qigong sessions chanting "Huu Hu" over and over again, a Sufi chant to open the heart. Then we would stand up, open our arms wide as if being crucified, and hold them in this position while taking long, slow, deep breaths—inhaling into the heart center and exhaling through the heart.

One Friday, as I lie in Corpse pose for deep relaxation, I saw an image of Mother Mary. She said, "Do you want to continue to play it safe? Or, risk opening your heart?" I said, "I no longer want to play it safe." I saw Mother Mary perform an operation on my heart, cutting my heart out of my body. It looked like surgery, blood and all, and then she replaced the old heart with a new heart. Of course, the operation was performed on my etheric body on the symbolic level, not on my physical body. At long last, my heart was healed.

Today, I have embarked on a new journey. I've retired as an engineer and continue to teach yoga weekly, but follow a new calling of my soul. My website Life As Yoga features the scope of yoga and metaphysical techniques that I learned and successfully used during my personal journey. My healing has taken over a dozen years and is still in progress, but I am now ready to heal others with the wisdom I gained. The knowledge does not make me a special person. It can be taught to others to enhance their lives. It's just a matter of doing the work. Our healing and growth cannot be rushed. It has to evolve naturally. The more we do the work—healing from our past and growing towards a more fulfilled individual—the lighter and brighter we become.

Catherine Kominos is the founder of VR Yogi, LLC, a start-up creating virtual reality meditation experiences. She has over thirty years of experience managing government research programs. She served in the Pentagon as the Deputy Director of Army Research, responsible for the oversight, management, and prioritization of the US Army basic research portfolio, with projects across twenty-three Army laboratories and sixteen Army-funded university centers. In addition, Catherine served as the Army's Congressional Fellow to Congressman Patrick Kennedy (D-R.I.), responsible for all legislative activities for the Department of Defense, Veteran's Affairs, and the House Armed Services Committee. As a director at the University of Southern California's Institute for Creative Technologies, Catherine generated millions of dollars in research collaborations with the US Army in robotics, virtual reality training, and neuroscience. *vryogi1@gmail.com*

21

Breck Pappas

Fake It till You Make It

I graduated from a small liberal arts university in Tennessee with a heart full of wanderlust and a bank account nearly empty of money. Like many before me, I chose the post-graduate get-rich-quick scheme. I got a job and moved back in with my parents.

The life of an office-dwelling proofreader took its toll and after a year, my windowless office felt more like a dungeon. When I had a few minutes to spare at work, I perused travel blogs and scrolled through hundreds of pictures of New Zealand. I wanted to live somewhere English-speaking and work outdoors and be active. I had a job but no other commitments—no mortgage and no girlfriend. I knew this was the only time in my life I would have this much freedom, and refused to let my life become defined by fluorescent lights and regret. Like jumping into a cold pool, I held my breath, ran, and leapt. I was twenty-four years old.

After only a few days in New Zealand, I was lucky to get a job offer. I would be working on the South Island for a business that takes customers out on the Pacific Ocean to swim with wild dolphins. Although I wouldn't be working on the boat, my job would be to help prepare the swimmers for their dolphin encounter and to clean and dry wetsuits. I was told that I wouldn't be needed for two months, and I liked the idea of playing New Zealand backpacker before settling down in one place for an extended period of time. Things seemed to be falling into place.

And then came the rude awakening.

I awoke with the usual new job jitters and forced myself to eat some toast and cereal in the spacious hostel kitchen. My hostel was about seven minutes by foot from work, but I allowed an extra five minutes just to be sure I didn't show up late on my first day. I dragged my feet forward along the sidewalk, not quite ready to commit myself to full-time employment again. It had been more than four months since I'd had a job. Although I had some good fun in those months, travel was more expensive than I had anticipated. In order to finance this adventure (and future ones), I needed to work. So there I was.

A stone's throw from the Pacific Ocean, I walked through the front doors and asked for the guy who would be training me. He led me down the hallway and through some double doors to a large, rectangular room that smelled of cleaning solution. On the left wall were countless flippers hanging on metal pegs in rows of blue, yellow, and black. Flipper sizes were scribbled on the bottom of each individual fin and arranged in an order that still wouldn't fully make sense days into my training. Next to the flippers on similar metal pegs hung black hoods, arranged by size: small, medium, and large. Next to the hoods was a rolling rack of masks and snorkels, organized in a way that required about five explanations from about four people before I quasi-understood how it all worked. And finally, the wetsuits. These were hung facing the same direction on seven rolling metal racks.

The first phase of my training required watching them suit up three boats of almost fifty dolphin swimmers with the correctly sized wetsuits. As they filed through the door in three groups, the swimmers were given a speech from one of the guides before stopping at each station to receive their equipment. When they got to us, my trainer effortlessly glided to a specific rack, selected the perfect wetsuit, and gave a three-second demonstration about putting it on correctly before sending the swimmer off to try it on in the changing room. The wetsuit fitting was an intimidating introduction to my job and a recipe for an awkward situation—especially when it came to correctly judging a girl's size. Having never worn a wetsuit before and having snorkeled only once, I wondered if I was the right person to be expertly fitting people with their equipment for a dolphin swim. The phrase "fake it till you make it" came to mind.

Once the three boats of swimmers were out the door, my training continued. That day is a blur. I'm talking like a trying-to-spot-an-ant-in-the-stands-from-the-passenger-seat-during-a-NASCAR-race blur. Before the swimmers left the property, I had to prepare a crate containing cookies, thermoses of hot chocolate, paper cups, and a jug of water for each boat. That involved checking with reservations for the updated swimmer counts to judge how much hot chocolate to make and which gear to lay out. I also had to radio out to the boats on the water, asking if they needed any spare equipment and if so, chuck it into the right crate for them to pick up when they got back.

Things really got interesting, though, in the washroom. A huge washing machine out back can clean six wetsuits at one time. After my trainer showed me the three separate buttons used to just get the machine on, he demonstrated how to fill it up with water and soap before stuffing it with the first load of wetsuits. After ninety seconds, the enormous drum stopped rotating and, one by one, he began taking the heavy, wet wetsuits from the machine and throwing them onto the floor of the washroom. From there, he hung each wetsuit on a metal rack, organized by male and female and then by size. It was a very wet job, and I suddenly discovered the source of the cleaning solution smell I had noticed earlier.

Cleaning and hanging up the wetsuits was the easy part. Drying them required skill. In order to effectively dry racks of wetsuits and get them ready for the next group of swimmers, you had to be strategic about their placement in the dry room. The Wetsuit Shuffle, as I called it, involves maneuvering racks of suits around in a tight place, placing the suits under fans and based on supply and demand, knowing which sized suits are more urgent to dry than others.

The many details of the job felt like learning a foreign language. Immersion is often the best way to become fluent, and I soon learned that my employers agreed with that belief. As my trainer explained, he would be going on vacation for the next few days. I would be running land duty for five days. I was overwhelmed with information my first few days of work, and I wondered more times than I'd like to admit, "What am I doing here?" I was buried in responsibility already and my training was over. The new employee manual didn't help much. The next day, I'd be in charge of cleaning and arranging all land equipment after one day of experience.

Trial by fire hardly begins to describe what those first few days were like for me. I struggled a lot and reevaluated my entire trip. I asked myself why I had come and if this was what I really wanted to do with my time in New Zealand. I hated those first few days of work. When I wasn't working, I was a nervous wreck thinking about work. Friends back home and even coworkers told me it would get better with time, but I wasn't acting like myself and I wasn't happy. Few times in my life could I remember being that unhappy.

I had decided to quit and move on with my adventure when one day, it all just kind of clicked. The things that I hated about the job didn't seem so bad, and it all just made a little more sense. I skyped my mom at the end of that day, "You know what? Today wasn't all that bad. I think I'm gonna try and stick this one out." Something felt different, but it was nothing about the job that changed. It was something within me that said, "OK, let's do this."

I now think that quitting that job would have been one of the biggest mistakes of my life, but I never would have known it if I had quit. At that crucial moment, two storylines were laid out for me.

1. When I moved to New Zealand, I got a job cleaning wetsuits and I hated it. I quit after a week.
2. When I moved to New Zealand, I got a job cleaning wetsuits. I hated it at first, but I stuck it out.

Looking back, I'm glad I didn't give up. I consider those months in New Zealand one of the most exciting, fulfilling times of my life. The people I met, the friendships I made, the beauty I witnessed, the things I tried, the confidence I gained will never be matched. I came to New Zealand to have new experiences and to see how far I could step outside my comfort zone. I decided the only thing to do was to strap on my wetsuit and hold on tight. Thank goodness I did.

Breck Pappas lived and worked in Kaikoura, New Zealand, for six months. He continued his travels throughout New Zealand, Australia, and Southeast Asia, before returning home to Mobile, Alabama. Breck is the senior writer for *Mobile Bay Magazine*.

22

Fotoula Adrimi

My Life Is More Than Stones and Mortar

My name is Fotoula Adrimi. I am a teacher of enlightened wisdom, including the healing path of ISET, the ancient Egyptian Mother Goddess, more commonly referred to as "ISIS"; ancient Egyptian spirituality; the Rays of Divine Consciousness; and shamanic healing. This is my story of how I came to own my spiritual gifts and discover my life purpose.

Early Childhood: Being One with God

I was born with gifts of clairvoyance, psychic awareness, inner knowing, and a deep well of wisdom and knowledge of right and wrong that I believe I brought from previous lives. Like many children, I came into this life with a direct connection to the spirit world, communicating with beings of light, the Divine, and the angelic realms. I felt supported and at one with the unseen world of spirit.

My Greek family has a lineage of psychic gifts. Various ancestors practiced the shamanic ways of herbal healing, bone divination, and the extraction of negative energies from a person's body. My father still practices bone divination, and my mother explains dreams. Despite this rich spiritual heritage, my parents revere science and deny the existence of the spirit world.

As a child, I was confused by the contradictory environment. My parents argued that if God could not be scientifically proven, he was an invention by needy souls looking for comfort in their desperate lives. How could one deny God's presence, as I was in direct communication with Him? I could feel and see God. I was in love with God. At school,

I enjoyed attending Mass and being bathed in the grace of God.

Every time I prayed, I could feel his incredibly loving presence around me. I have an early memory of seeing God's smiling face, reassuring me and protecting me from danger. I believe God saved my life several times as a child, including once being pulled back when I ran to cross the road. Time stopped, and so did I. A car shot past.

When I was nine, Mother Mary (who plays a vital role in the Greek Orthodox religion) started coming to me. Jesus's Mother is the lady of compassion, who performs miracles to alleviate suffering. Mother Mary became what I would now call "my spiritual guide." When I wanted something, I would ask Mother Mary, and she would grant it. I would ask to win raffles at school, and I did. These were the innocent requests of a child. I was very happy. I could see angels, and all my prayers were answered. I had no fear and a huge trust in God.

I was fascinated by a book on ancient Egypt and wanted to go. Living in Kavala, Greece, I would sit on my balcony and gaze at the Aegean Sea, knowing that on the other side of these waters lay a sacred land. In daydreams, I would fly over the sea to the ancient temples and the Valley of the Kings, accompanied by a radiant woman, whom I later discovered was the Egyptian goddess and being of light known as "ISET" (or more commonly, "ISIS"). In Herodotus's *The Histories* and Plato's dialogues *Timaeus and Critias*, I read about Atlantis and intuitively knew I had also once lived there. I never told my parents.

Teen Years: Parting from Grace

In grade school, I realized how different I was from other children. I once shared with a classmate how Mother Mary helped me tell the time. Then other classmates started telling me I should not concern Mother Mary with something "so trivial." I also began to feel guilty for winning so many raffles because Mother Mary was intervening on my behalf, whilst others did not have this gift. I returned the last prize, but could not tell the headmaster why.

In high school, I still felt the presence of spirits, but I started to fear them. A classmate's mother told me the church regards psychic experiences as devil's work. In desperation, I spoke to the priest, who said it was a great sin to meddle with these things. Still, I did not speak to my parents about what was happening. From being a happy child surrounded by the love of spirit, I was starting to doubt myself. I now believed it was wrong to talk to spirits, and I grew sad and alone.

Young Adulthood: Leading a "Normal" Life

The more I distanced myself from spirit, the less psychic I became. I focused instead on university exams and everyday life. I feared anything abnormal or unexplainable. At the University of Thessaly in Volos, I studied town planning as my parents advised, rather than following my heart to learn ancient Greek and philosophy. They argued that town planning would allow me to make a good living and join the family business.

Despite feeling powerless to choose my major, I enjoyed the course, won two scholarships, and after graduation, I pursued a master's degree at the Sorbonne in Paris. There I met my future husband. We were young and fell madly in love. After finishing my degree, I moved to Scotland to be with him, and we wed. I did what society expected: I studied to get a job, met a man, and married.

We moved into a house built in the mid-1800s that was full of dead people (spirits who had passed but not moved on). When I was alone in the outbuildings, I felt the spirit presences come to me like a force of energy. My old fears, which had begun in high school, resurfaced. I would recite the Lord's Prayer, but the spirits were persistent. One morning, my husband and I awoke to the manual alarm on the backdoor, which could only be activated by someone physically opening the door. Yet no one had been there. The door was locked from the inside.

I now know that these spirits were trying to attract my attention so I could help them pass over to the spiritual realm. They could see the light in me and were attracted to it. I still had too much fear of the spirit world then and ran away from it.

Returning to the Gift

I was immersed in a conventional life, commuting three hours each day to my job as a town planner, staying in the office from nine to five, rushing home to cook dinner, and then vegetating in front of the TV. My husband and I had grown apart, and I felt stuck in a loveless marriage. Stressed and tired, I felt dead to life.

Then I turned thirty and was drawn back into the spiritual world and back into life. I always had had an excellent memory, but my memory was noticeably less sharp. At the library, I checked out a book called *Mind Magic*, written in 1991 by medium Betty Shine, thinking it was a book on memory. Everything in *Mind Magic* spoke to me. The spiritual truths Betty described, I knew to be true. I had witnessed similar events as a child. Yes, it was OK to speak to spirits. Yes, it was normal. What a revelation.

Betty explained how one can heal a person or an animal by visualizing blue light surrounding him. I decided to experiment on Shep, the family dog, who had a tumor and was due for an operation. In my mind, I pictured Shep and tried to see the blue light. I was focusing and calling forth this blue light. Suddenly, I saw a streak of blue light coming from my right and onto the image of Shep in my mind. The blue light was not imagined. I was visualizing the dog, but I saw the blue light with my eyes. I knew then that the dog would be fine and get well. The next day, Shep's tumor was a quarter of its original size. I repeated the exercise that evening, saw a less intense streak of blue light coming from my right side. The next day, the tumor was gone. I believe the dog took on this illness only so that I could finally wake up and step into my spiritual path.

I started reading about the healing properties of crystals. I attempted meditations on chakras (the main energy centers of the body) by lying down and placing crystals of the appropriate color on my chakras and emptying my mind. These exercises not only gave me incredible peace but also showed me the imbalances in my everyday life and how much I had compromised my own happiness to please others. I was becoming aware of the bigger picture, rather than simply living an aimless life.

When I returned the book, the library assistant asked me if I had been to the Stirling Spiritualist Church. She explained that the congregation meets weekly, and a medium offers evidence of life after death and even tells members of the audience about their dead relatives. I summoned the courage to go. I sat at the back and held onto my cross, just in case the devil popped out from the corner. The medium never came to me.

I returned to the church and this time, I sat in the middle section. The next time, I sat in the front row. I became more comfortable and less fearful. An announcement was made that people who wanted to try channeling their deceased relatives could come to a circle night. We all sat in a circle and opened in prayer and sang hymns. Then while listening to some relaxation music, we closed our eyes for ten minutes and asked the spirits to come to us. Despite my ease with the practice, I had little success.

We tried again for another ten minutes. This time, I saw myself happy and swimming in the sea. In another vision I was in Africa, watching a wooden house being built. I saw beautiful, wooden carvings delivered to the house and carefully packed to be sent abroad to Scotland. When we shared what we had seen, the woman next to me confirmed that she had once lived in an African country, where she had built a wooden house. Upon leaving Africa, she ordered some wooden carvings, which she brought with her to Scotland. I had seen something that someone else could verify.

Getting in touch with the spirit world and my true essence helped me to calm the mind and release fear and expectations. I had started practicing meditation and mindfulness, and realized I had some difficult personal decisions to make. I chose to separate from my husband. No matter what happened to me as a newly divorced, working woman,

I learned to let go of the anger and find inner peace. This was a time of great self-empowerment. I lived in an expensive home, had a secure salary, and my ex-husband had a good job—but this material wealth did not make me happy. I was not prepared to waste my life for stones and mortar.

Training in the Healing and Spiritual Arts

I wanted to rediscover my gifts in a disciplined and grounded way. Now living in Glasgow, I enrolled at the Theosophical Society in spiritual development classes designed to help people get in touch with their spirit guides. My ability to converse with God and Mother Mary was still there, but I had to learn to know when and how to use it.

I trained in all sorts of vibrational and energetic healing methods, including Reiki. And then, I found shamanism. In 2007 (two years after I first attended the church in Stirling), I went to a shamanic workshop, although I didn't know then what "shamanic" meant. Shamanism is a spiritual practice where we merge or work with spirits to journey in realities parallel to our own, for healing, guidance, and divination on behalf of our clients and ourselves.

I learned how to journey. As soon as I closed my eyes, a Native American spirit man appeared and asked me to follow him. I took to shamanism like a fish to water, training as a shamanic practitioner. In America, I studied with Sandra Ingerman.

When I opened up to my spiritual path, my life completely changed. I had so much energy. I was working full-time as a senior planning officer for the City of Glasgow and running a private healing consultancy evenings and weekends. Healing work made my heart sing.

Channel of ISIS: My Gift to the World

We all come into the world with unique gifts, but sometimes we see our gifts and run away. Early on my healing path, ISIS (or ISET), the ancient Egyptian Mother Goddess, known as the "divine mother of unconditional love," came to me. In 2006, I woke up with the bed shaking and moving side to side due to an energy column of light entering my body. The experience was physical—not a dream, and I felt no fear, only curiosity. As I shifted my body away from the energy column, the bed's shaking and moving intensified. I realized that I should put myself back underneath the column. Then I blacked out. I later learned ISIS was embedding the blueprint of the ISIS teachings I was going to channel as well as the program for my future life.

That year, ISIS asked me to visit Egypt, where an energy of light (divine consciousness) still emanates from many of the sacred sites. Inside the Great Pyramid, I started climbing the "Great Gallery," the narrow and steep corridor leading to the King's Chamber. I could feel the weight of the huge blocks around me. ISIS came, and I chanted some of her sacred songs that I had channeled but to no effect. My spirit guides kept telling me to center myself.

After an hour, I climbed down the corridor. I heard psychically some sounds being chanted over and over. They were simple sounds but put together, made a song. Unconsciously, I started singing this chant. I felt a rush of energy from the ceiling and the walls, all around me. The pyramid was coming alive. I felt exuberant and kept singing. My guides said this chant with the right intention is the key that unlocks the Great Pyramid, and was my initiation into my spiritual power. Initiation is a process of attunement, where the light flows into our body to open our spiritual channels and raises our vibration, helping to increase our awareness.

Bringing the Gift to the World

ISIS gave me a teaching called the "Seven Gates of Awareness," which is about becoming enlightened. Spirituality is not about one's ability to see spirits; it is about experiencing the vastness and eternity of one's own soul and light, and the manifestation of this light into the world for the highest good of all. We each have to face and overcome the obstacles of our mind and our doubts and fears.

Personal work takes effort. I do a lot of inner work to be as pure a channel as possible. ISIS shows me how my ego manifests and how fine the line is between acting out of love and acting out of fear. I keep working on myself, transforming the mind into the wisdom of the heart. I gave up alcohol, my planning job, toxic relationships, and even TV. I meditate daily. I connect with ISIS daily. This is my job now. This is my life.

My Self-Healing

In 2015, I participated in a death and dying vision quest, and I learned to trust in life. In a vision quest ceremony, one fasts four days and four nights out in the wild. On the third night while asleep, I was bitten by an insect. It must have been a horsefly, because I am allergic to horseflies and awoke in a lot of pain. My lower lip must have become infected as it was swelling rapidly. I was having an allergic reaction and had no emergency drugs, no antibiotics, and no homeopathic medicine.

All I had was the ISIS healing energies I work with. I started channeling them through the crown of my head, directing them to my lower lip and then my hands were lit, as if they were channeling a gentle, warm fire. As I placed my hands close to my face, I saw inside my lip. There was black space and a little black ball, which I identified as the poison from the horsefly. I saw strands of blue light flowing and surrounding the black ball. The vision then stopped. I knew that I was healed even though my lip still hurt. The inner voice said, "You are healed." Exhausted, I fell asleep and woke up a couple of hours later. The swelling was gone completely. There was no mark, nothing on my face.

My spirit guides and teachers of the light said we are able to heal ourselves through light. We are all light, but our human conditioning prevents us from experiencing our luminosity and radiance. These ancient ceremonies and teachings have helped me to reconnect with my true essence. May we all awaken into the sphere of eternal light within.

Fotoula Adrimi, BA(Hons), MSc, is the director of the ISIS School of Holistic Health, an international school of healing arts, spiritual development, and inner transformation through vibrational energy work, enlightened teachings, shamanism, and meditation. She is part of the global network of Shamanic Teachers under Sandra Ingerman. Fotoula lives and works in Glasgow, Scotland, has taught in Germany and the Netherlands, and has led spiritual pilgrimages to Egypt. Her first book, *The Golden Book of Wisdom: Ancient Spirituality and Shamanism for Modern Times*, an Amazon UK bestseller, is an epitome of spiritual learning, mysticism, and soul evolution.
theisisschoolofholistichealth.com

23

Sheri Lynn

I Have Been to Hell and Learned to Thrive

It's December, and I am on a quiet, public beach in Mexico—not part of a resort. I'm sitting in the sand sipping hot coffee that I made on a camp stove. My coffee contains a generous dose of Kahlúa. In a haze, I'm watching whales and dolphins swim by. A small part of my brain realizes this is a majestic sight; the rest of my brain is simply numb. My middle child Graham, my son of sixteen, is standing in a deep hole buried up to his neck in sand. He spent hours digging this hole. I put a hat on his head to protect him from the sun, and occasionally he calls out for help to smoke a cigarette. When I remember, I pour water into his mouth to keep him hydrated.

It is legal for my eighteen-year-old daughter, Cameron, to drink here. She had spent much of the night vomiting tequila through her woven hammock and woke up in the soiled sand, having fallen out. She is nursing her hangover with Corona and crying for Marshal. Marshal was my youngest. Fourteen years old, and dead two? three? four? weeks earlier of a self-inflicted gunshot wound in our home in New Mexico.

Since Marshal's death, I had been seriously suicidal. I was so scared for him. I didn't know where he was, how he would navigate, who would be taking care of him. I wanted to protect him in death as I had in life. Yes, yes, yes, there are all the pat answers about God and Heaven and all of that, and none of it was making sense to me. In fact the reassurances I was receiving from others only angered me. "How do you *know*?" I would ask. The pitying looks on their faces drove me insane. It seemed to me that there were a wide variety of things we humans can tell ourselves when the sh*t hits the fan. And the things

I told myself in order to survive changed hour by hour. Whatever it took. I knew I had no faith in any of it. My brother, who had been staying with us in New Mexico, hid the kitchen knives and anything else he thought I could harm myself with. I was too tired to be creative.

The kids and I had piled into my dark blue family van and drove to this deserted Mexican beach to avoid the onslaught of Christmas, the holiday most fraught with emotions. I don't even remember whose idea it was. Having crossed the border, we were pulled over by government officials with machine guns. I was not afraid. My Spanish was not good enough for the interaction. It seemed not to matter.

And here we were. On this beach, drinking and smoking and crying and vomiting and wandering and being held together by wet sand and grief over Marshal. Through the dizzying details of the death, the funeral, the family, the well-meaning folks bearing strange casseroles and alcohol, I did not drink. I did not leave my bed much. I do not remember all that went on, but the pastor from Marshal's church told me whatever I did, not to drink or it would be harder on me later. And so I didn't. Now I did, here, about a month later, on this beach.

Sitting with the grief pounding me, I was terrified. How do I look normal? How do I speak in a way that makes sense? How do I get back to caring? How do I keep up the constant stream of stories in my head to placate myself into living another hour? People say to me that it is "unimaginable to lose a child." I agree. I lost a child, and it is still unimaginable to me. The pain is bottomless. There is no way to get my arms around it. No way to contain it. No way to describe it. Years later, I can say that I learned to live with it in a way that others are comfortable. It still can bring me to my knees without warning. I have come to understand Marshal's suicide was a gaping hole blown through me. I have learned to live with the hole.

There on the beach, back to the beach, the only way out I knew of was to die. And yet dribbling water into Graham's mouth or lighting his cigarettes, holding Cameron's head in my lap and stroking her hair,

I asked myself, "Who would tend to these children?" "How would they survive?" I argued with myself that they were old enough. Sure enough, they were. I paced in the surf. I could wander out, out to where it was deep, and just let myself go under. I could. I would. I imagined that. I emotionally experienced it. Again, my attention was drawn back to my son and daughter. I thought of them losing their mother so quickly after losing their brother and after having lost their father ten years earlier, and while I knew that in some way they would survive, I could not be responsible for that.

For the next two years, I contemplated dying and I contemplated living. I was living in hell and swimming in grief and faking it on every level. I engaged in self-destructive behaviors, especially in the beginning. Then for another year every Saturday morning, I wrote in my journal, thought, and cried. I reached inside fearlessly and gave myself a thorough going-over. I recognized my slow suicidal path, and I needed to respond. Slowly I arrived at a plan.

Were I to choose life, my life had to be worthwhile on some level. I had to learn to live in a way that was different from what I had known. I had to find a way to not just survive, but to nourish myself and thrive. I had to contribute to others in some way. Finally I drafted a five-year plan for living, goals for my life that, at the time, felt beyond what I was capable of. I met every goal. Then I set new goals. And exceeded those.

I started with my physical fitness and health. I got moving, which was a crucial part of my transformation. By agreeing to not off myself, I needed to also agree to treat my body as if I wanted it to live. I also understood that no one else was going to love me to health. I was going to have to love myself to health, and basic self-care is how my body knows I love and appreciate it.

As my physical health improved, so did my emotional health. As my body became stronger, my thinking became clearer. I confronted my resistance to taking care of myself. Caring for my health brought me back to my mental aspect and then opened my heart. The turning point came from all those Saturday mornings spent navel-gazing, when I decided to live and to help others.

My personal story soon became very public. As I changed my body, people asked me for help. I did, and then more people asked me. I earned a personal training certification and switched careers (I had been a minerals engineer). Right away I was busy. I developed a biomechanical system of movement to help people in pain and provide them with a way to change their bodies through food. In 2006, I founded Genesis Transformation, a personal empowerment business. Our motto is "the body achieves what the mind believes," and so the first step is a self-appraisal of your beliefs.

I live this work. I have a passion for it. I believe that teaching others to love and care for themselves, to take responsibility for their health and their lives, is discouraged in our culture. Typical American marketing messages are "go on this diet," "trust the TV," "take these drugs," "eat this." We come to believe that we do not have what it takes to thrive. I am here to tell you that you do: You have within you what it takes to thrive. It is inherent in being human. You have the right to thrive.

Genesis Transformation appeals mainly to women between thirty-five and sixty-five, for whom nothing has worked; yet, they are determined to find a way to thrive. They understand that they are being fed a lot of cr*p by the tens-of-billions-of-dollars-a-year diet industry, and they don't know whom to trust. They see my clients' results and harbor some hope. They learn how to take care of themselves. They learn that only you can fix you. Yes, they get an amazingly fit body; however, they also get what comes with it: the ability to thrive. And you can, too.

My personal transformation work and the business I founded came from my depths. I have been to hell, and I have learned to thrive. I have learned to transform myself over and over to meet life on a level where I can flourish. I have found joy and compassion and have lived to be grateful for what Marshal has taught me in his death. Do not ask me to say it was worth it.

Sheri Lynn is an independent educator and a human transformation artist. She raised three children and is the grandmother of thirteen. Sheri lives in Montana, and believes that a good deal of her time is best spent knitting.

24

Arlene Faulk

A Gentle Reminder

For nineteen years, I had a successful career with a Fortune 100 corporation and never said anything about my physical challenges. I hid severe physical pain, loss of mobility, and numbness in my hands and feet that I had quietly lived with for decades.

Then, one morning in my office, I was working at my computer when a sudden wave of exhaustion permeated my brain. My head bobbed forward. I leaned over and placed my head in the palms of my hands. Weakness drained every ounce of strength from my arms. Needle-like pain ran up my right leg. Like kryptonite crippling Superman, this amorphous fatigue rendered me completely weak and vulnerable. Somehow I managed to drive the twenty-five miles from the office to my home.

I believed this sudden attack was temporary. Surely in a few days the fatigue would pass and my executive's life would resume. Day three, I dragged myself off my couch, crept out of my condo door, and rode downstairs in the elevator. Disoriented, I hoped the fresh air might revive me. Outside, I turned right and walked half a block. Suddenly, I needed to lie down.

Back in my condo, I spent the rest of the day flat on my back. In the past, I had always been able to push beyond my physical limitations. This was different. No matter how hard I tried, my body said, "No."

Then I laid down on my living room couch, and didn't get up. For two years. The pain was chronic and increasing in severity. I went on long-term disability from my employer.

At the time my good friend Amy was seeing an acupuncturist and bodyworker. "Nancy Floy is helping me to connect my busy mind with my body, and I feel great," Amy said enthusiastically. "Why don't you make an appointment with her, Arlene?"

"I'll think about it," I said. I had always been a problem-solver, a do-er, a person who had always come up with multiple options. Day after day, I kept thinking and analyzing. My trusted mind that had served me so well for many years was not producing (perhaps fogged by the drugs to mitigate fatigue and reduce inflammation).

Perhaps I didn't act on Amy's suggestion because "acupuncturist" and "bodyworker" were foreign to me. I was a skeptic with roots in Western medicine: my father was a family physician and my older brother, a gastroenterologist. I examined my life as it was, but I couldn't figure out the next step. My mind kept trying to solve my body pains without paying attention to what my body wanted. The medicines to reduce fatigue were ineffective, and my neurologist said, "There's nothing more I can do for you."

Several months later, an envelope arrived in the mail. Inside, Amy had written "A Gentle Reminder" and attached Nancy's business card. Immediately, I got up from the couch and called Nancy to schedule an appointment.

At our first meeting, Nancy gave me a massage. She encouraged me to appreciate how much my body had been through and for so long and also to nurture myself. For the next two years, I saw Nancy every other week for an hour and a half, and sometimes more frequently, if I had a relapse and once again lost my ability to walk. I listened carefully as she talked about qi (life-force energy) and meridians (pathways) and TCM (traditional Chinese medicine). Nancy suggested I listen and talk to my body. I didn't understand what she was saying.

Each treatment entailed Nancy using her hands and fingers to find and apply pressure to specific points on my body. In our third session, she added acupuncture needles to further stimulate these points. Within an hour after the acupuncture treatment ended, I felt a little chill. Much of the pain and aching in my legs had vanished. Four hours later, at home, the pain in my legs returned and quickly intensified. My legs felt like they were plugged into an electric socket. By phone, Nancy directed me to where to apply pressure.

That pattern continued. I would see Nancy, feel a huge decrease in pain and numbness, experience better balance, and then lose ground a few hours afterward. I was frustrated. Some days, I questioned whether this difficult work was worth it. Was I making any progress? Determined to keep trying, I stuck with it. By this time, I believed in Nancy and felt she really cared. She was a cheerleader for my body and saw me as a whole person—not as an illness or a condition to treat. She was unique.

Slowly, over a year, I began to have breakthroughs, hours when my pain decreased. The hours turned into days. After a year and a half, good days became good weeks.

Four months into my treatment sessions, Nancy suggested I try Tai Chi. Although I was only forty-seven years old at the time, I signed up for a Tai Chi class with seniors. As the teacher demonstrated how to stand and walk with proper alignment, I clutched my cane self-consciously. Gingerly, I moved to a spot next to the wall for added support. This is how my Tai Chi experience started. For eighteen months, in addition to attending class, I practiced a daily walking exercise in my hallway.

Frankly I didn't know what I was ready for. I just jumped off the cliff. Neither Nancy nor I knew what the course of my multiple sclerosis would be. Nine years after my initial attack, I had received the tentative diagnosis of MS, confirmed by MRI twelve years later (twenty-one years after onset).

If I had known where I would be today, I would not have believed it. Today I enjoy robust health, walk with a lilt in my step, and am off all medications. I am at a place I did not know was possible. My work with Nancy was my most challenging effort ever. I kept with it and her, even on days when I didn't want to. That hard work was instrumental in my healing. I'm convinced that we must be an active participant in the effort to heal, with inspiration, support, and professional expertise from outside sources. I am convinced because I personally have been such a participant. Tai Chi helped to reinforce and expand the positive effects that I had with Nancy.

I began teaching Tai Chi in 1999. In every class, I teach and practice walking in proper alignment. The opportunity to teach Tai Chi, which has helped transform my life, is an honor. Many of my students face daily health challenges, painful chronic conditions such as arthritis, back pain, lupus, fibromyalgia, MS, Parkinson's, and anxiety. I encourage each student to start where he or she is: "Bring your attention to your body. Do only what you can do. Give yourself permission to sit down for a few minutes if you need to." I tell my class, "Be aware of your body and note anything you're feeling, without judging it. Just note it and let it go for the next hour."

Gentle reminders. Soft encouragement. They have been important in my healing, and I try to give that back to my students.

I hope my story inspires and gives hope to readers by expanding their knowledge of options for healing. I wish that readers facing a chronic health condition may find a new direction. Today I celebrate each day and am grateful to be able to walk.

Arlene Faulk founded Faulk Tai Chi in 1999 and teaches in Chicago and Evanston, Illinois. After a successful corporate career in human resources, despite formidable physical hurdles with multiple sclerosis (MS), she transformed her life through Tai Chi and Qigong. Arlene feels grateful every day to be able to walk and to help others embrace change through Tai Chi. In 2022, Arlene published *Walking on Pins and Needles: A Memoir of Chronic Resilience in the Face of Multiple Sclerosis*, her story of perseverance, rediscovery, and hope.
arlenefaulk.com

Nancy Floy, LAc., MA, Dipl.Ac., an acupuncturist and bodyworker, founded and is co-director of Heartwood Integrative Health and Healing, a collective committed to providing excellence in integrative health services, classes, and events in Evanston, Illinois.
heartwoodcenter.com

25

K. B.

Just Be

My miracle is of a spiritual awakening. Some would say that the miracle is life itself, because on December 25, 2012, at age forty-seven, I woke up. I woke up from a drug- and alcohol-induced state that should have killed me. As much a blessing it is to have survived my suicide attempt, more miraculous is the re-awakening of my spirit.

For many years I struggled with feeling not good enough.

Having been adopted as a child, I have attachment issues. I believed my birth mother gave me up because I was a mistake. I learned from a young age to please my adoptive parents. I didn't want to be given away again. I also craved attention. I confused pleasing others and receiving attention with love. I learned how to work hard, please, and perform to get the love I wanted. Having grown up middle-class in a rich suburb in Minneapolis where everyone else looked perfect and drove perfect cars and lived in perfect houses, I developed a poor body image. In sixth grade, a beautiful girl told me that I "was not fat, [I] was chubby."

Going off to college, I was locked and loaded to use academic success to feel better. I was the first kid from my family to go to college, and I was determined to succeed and go to law school. But I still I felt unworthy, lonely, and empty. I joined a sorority. I tried to fill the emptiness with food and later with alcohol. After bingeing the first year, I switched to bingeing and purging. Of course I would feel even worse after the purging, but that wouldn't stop me from repeating the cycle. I gained the freshman fifteen (or in my case, the freshman twenty-five).

With the newfound freedom of college, I also tried turning to men and romance to fill that need for attention and to feel OK about myself. I was a virgin when I left for college, which was the norm in my world. I was not able to date in high school. Having been raised in a traditional Greek Orthodox family and its faith, I learned that you needed to be a virgin when you got married. Else, you were damaged goods.

I wanted to be wanted. I wanted attention. I noticed a cute guy who paid attention to me and bought me drinks. A bunch of us sorority sisters went back to the fraternity for a dance in their basement. My sorority sisters thought it was "wrong" that I was still a virgin—after all, I was in college. In just a few hours of attention from this cute guy I already had a crush on him. I was hoping we would get to dance together, with maybe even a slow dance and possibly a kiss.

After drinking and dancing, we ended up in his fraternity house dorm room. I was terribly naïve but I just wanted to continue to bask in more of that wonderful warm feeling of attention I was getting from him. We kissed. I was on cloud nine, in heaven. I felt wanted. I fell asleep in his arms while thinking it had been the most romantic night of my life. I woke up some time later to him raping me. I cried. I asked him to stop. I begged. I couldn't move, as I felt like all my limbs were too heavy to move. He told me I would like it and to enjoy it. I told him I was a virgin and needed to be a virgin when I got married. I begged him to stop. He did not stop.

The year after the rape was the first time I considered suicide. When I returned to the sorority after the party, not really sure how I got there, I hid in a closet and cried for hours. I assumed I would get pregnant, and I could not live with that. I tried talking to my sorority-sister roommate, but her response was, "It's about time you are not a virgin. Get over it." I tried going to the priest for help, who asked me what I had been wearing and told me I "would be forgiven." I tried talking to my mom, who fell to the ground in a dramatic manner raising her arms to ask God, "Where did [she] go wrong?"

More than ever before, I felt like I was a mistake. I turned to alcohol to drown myself. While I was using alcohol I engaged in risky behavior with men. I conquered them, having sex and separating myself emotionally so as to show the world and myself that nothing could hurt me. Through all my self-destructive behavior and acting out, I still excelled in school. It was the one thing I could still hold onto that fed my self-worth. Performing well also led to positive attention from my parents. I don't remember much of that first year, and it is a miracle that I survived.

Also my freshman year, I met my birth mother. When I was with the priest receiving confession for rape and praying I would meet my birth mother, the Children's Home Society that had placed me nineteen years before was calling my home. They had found my birth mother. I didn't see it then as another miracle, but I do now. Meeting my birth mother was something that I thought would fill the curiosity and emptiness I had felt growing up. I was so excited to see that I look like her and to learn about many traits we share.

My growing attachment to my birth mother was uncomfortable for my adoptive mom, and to spare her feelings, I kept my visits with my birth mother secret. Feeling pulled apart at the seams, I did what I knew how to do. I ran. I applied to law schools only on the East and West coasts.

During my first semester of law school in Oregon, living almost two thousand miles from anyone I knew, I grew lonelier. The transition was also rough because earlier years of schooling had come easy. This was not. By the end of the first semester, my bulimia caught up with me, and I landed in the hospital (after I had finished finals). From the binging, purging, and massive amounts of alcohol and ibuprofen, I had put a hole in my stomach.

To earn my right to leave the hospital I agreed to group therapy for the bulimia. Although a size four and an average weight, I perceived my body as huge. Group therapy was eventually successful in stopping the cycle of my binging and purging, but didn't touch my underlying feelings of unworthiness. I had picked up a new coping mechanism: compulsive exercise.

After graduation I returned home, passed the bar, and got engaged. The problems I had fled from were waiting for me. The issues with my mother and birth mother resurfaced when I was creating the wedding guest list. Going into marriage, I had high hopes for the romance that we had created. Certainly through this love affair, I thought I would feel alright. My happily-ever-after romantic fantasy was as good as any novelist could write. We honeymooned in the Greek islands and over the years, enjoyed many overseas trips.

In time tensions flared, and as I had done in childhood, I gauged others' moods and acted accordingly to maintain the peace. Pregnant with our first child, we had a bitter argument one evening. And for the second time in my life, suicide started swirling about in my head. I was sitting in the tub and imagined blood seeping out of my wrists. As a good Greek Orthodox girl, marriage was supposed to be forever. Somehow, I summoned up the courage to break the rules. Nine years and two kids, a son and a daughter, later, the marriage ended in divorce.

One of the best parts of the end of my marriage was the beginning of my counseling. I began to work on connecting with myself, being the woman I most wanted to be, and making authentic choices. The hardest concept of all was the thought of loving myself. Along this positive road of personal development, at the urging of my therapist, I even stopped drinking. I had met a kind, brilliant man coming out of the porta-potty at a horse show, and eventually we married. I had achieved great success in my field as a lawyer. We had bought a horse farm and were enjoying living our dream.

When the economy collapsed in 2008, things started to unravel. As day-to-day life got more challenging, my food and alcohol consumption increased. My daily glass of wine frequently became a daily bottle. Nothing I did could fill the hole. I felt like I was in a hole of quicksand, and I was losing the battle. I felt completely worthless.

Then a few events occurred starting summer 2012 that pushed me over the edge. My dad was diagnosed with terminal cancer and died; we never got to say good-bye. My husband was in a freak horsing accident and once home from the hospital, required my full-time care. Since I wasn't able to work either, our financial obligations were mounting. Many of my old buried feelings of unworthiness came screaming back.

I don't remember what the last straw was. I felt I was not good enough—as a consoling daughter to my grieving mother, a nurturing wife to my convalescing husband, a loving mother to my young kids, and a good wage earner. I felt like no matter what I did and for whom, I couldn't please anyone. I didn't want to be a bother any more. I felt terribly alone, and I was also really tired. None of my survival and coping skills seemed to be working any more. For the first time in my life, I was underperforming. It was dark and terrifying. I started researching how to take my life.

Confiding in others after the rape and toward the end of my first marriage, I was denied any compassion and help. I learned to hide, and I was hiding from everyone—even my therapist. I put my plan into action on Christmas 2012. I sent everyone texts to remind them that I loved them. And then I took two different prescription drugs meant to depress my breathing and drank massive amounts of scotch.

I was surprised, and moreover angry, when I woke up hours later in the hospital. "I have failed even at taking my life." All I wanted was to go home and try to kill myself again. The hospital recommended a three-day lockup in a mental institution. For three days, all I had to do was just be and talk to people. I read and exercised. I started to care for myself and consider myself in small but significant ways. I asked one of the counselors if I "had a right to be happy?"

When I left the hospital, I was still at an all-time low. I restarted weekly therapy and began attending weekly Alcoholics Anonymous (A.A.) meetings. I started to connect with God again and to connect with myself. One of the hardest exercises for me was to look in the mirror and recite the "I Love You" prayer. "I love you, I love you, I love you. I have always loved you. Live each day to the fullest and know that my spirit will always be with you." I had never felt worthy of love.

I began to work through the twelve steps. At first I was the cynical person in the corner, there because she had to be but who did not think she had a problem. As I listened to others' stories and started working the program, I became more grateful for the small things again—like nature. I found comfort in the belief that no matter what was swirling around me that I had no control over, I could be who I wanted to be within it. When I felt physical pain I would tell myself, feeling pain is better than not feeling. When I was sad, I would say, experiencing emotions again is better than anesthetizing them.

Each day is a gift and all I really have. I start each day with A.A. readings and A.A. meditations where I feel joy and celebrate life. As the day progresses I frequently get off track and feel crabby, despondent, or down. I am human. Some days are better than others. But even on the worst days, I feel a light, a warmth. I no longer act out in self-destructive ways. I no longer feel like I am a mistake. I no longer confuse pleasing others and receiving attention with love. I see the child within who needs and deserves my love. More than anything, I know I am not alone in the dark. I know I am loved. And that is my miracle.

K. B. is a lawyer practicing in Minneapolis, Minnesota.

26

Madge Lockwood

Jane's Ascent

Madge Lockwood and I met by luck. My naturopath had recommended that I start a detoxification program, incorporating regular manual lymph drainage (MLD) treatments. I chose Madge because her office was closest to my home. From my first step as Jane the Explorer and through my physical challenges, setbacks, and victories, Madge has been my healing partner. She has also served as a mirror to my progress—something I would often lose sight of when focused on my daily grind of staying alive. Madge was as committed to continuing her education here and abroad as I was to healing myself. What are the odds that I'd meet a professional learning German techniques little known in the States but uniquely suited for my health issues? Although her methods may not be appropriate for every one, Madge's objective view of my recovery can serve as an example of a productive and successful healing partnership, and may inspire you to search for your own Madge.

—Jane G. Doyle

In January 2009, Jane Doyle came to me for manual lymph drainage (MLD) treatments for detoxification and to support her immune system and adrenal glands. She had digestive issues and suffered from constant headaches, frequent sinus infections and colds, and chronic neck, hip, knee, and ankle pain. Jane was committed to finding alternative and holistic methods to get healthy and pain-free without pharmaceuticals or surgery. I am one of several practitioners who have accompanied Jane on her journey.

MLD uses rhythmic strokes to increase lymphatic flow. The gentle movements stimulate the lymph vessels to contract, which allow more waste products, proteins, and excess fluid to be removed from the body's tissues into the lymphatic system. The lymphatic system transports fluids between the tissues and the bloodstream and protects the body from infection and disease through the immune response system. MLD can speed the healing from injury and surgery by reducing swelling and inflammation, boost the immune system, and benefit many other conditions such as lymphedema, autoimmune disorders, headaches, and Lyme disease.

Jane and I soon added orthopedic massage (OM) to address her neck pain, stemming from a head-on collision about thirty years earlier. OM involves assessment with orthopedic tests, manual therapy, and movement to resolve pain and dysfunction from traumatic injuries, overuse, and postural imbalances. I trained in two types of OM. Marnitz Therapy centers on stimulating the neurofunctional chains in the body to unwind long held pain patterns. The other technique focuses on ligament and tendon strains and injuries.

After Jane completed the eight MLD treatments recommended by her naturopath, we addressed the other musculoskeletal problems with myofascial therapy and Kinesio taping. Myofascial therapy is an oil-free, deep tissue technique that uses slow, engaging strokes to release restricted fascia of the muscles. Fascia is the connective tissue that surrounds all muscles and organs in the body. Tight and dehydrated muscles can stick to neighboring muscles and structures, and cause pain. The therapy unwinds these restrictions to restore full function. Jane also benefited from the European version of Kinesio taping, which was developed by the U.S.-trained Japanese chiropractor Kenzo Kase as a less invasive method to treat soft tissue (i.e., muscle and ligament) injuries and improve fluid movement (i.e., lymph and blood). Taping also produces sensory feedback to help activate the body's healing process.

June 2009, Jane started a weekly yoga class. Unable to sit comfortably in Hero pose (i.e., on bent legs resting on her heels and the tops of her feet), she had a rough start. At first, I was lymph taping Jane's ankles, knees, hips, sacrum, low back, and neck—scheduled around her yoga classes. Taping, usually kept on five days, became key to help support Jane's ligaments and muscles while she slowly built strength and flexibility and kept her free from neck, low back, and ankle pain while her body healed. Consistent yoga practice slowly opened up the ankle joint to where the pose no longer caused pain.

February 2010, Jane began seeing an osteopath, who performed neck adjustments to align her cervical vertebra (to relieve her headaches) and started her on the human chorionic gonadotropin (HCG) diet (to reset her metabolism). Jane alternated between the osteopath and me and continued to practice yoga. Soon, we were taping only one ankle, one knee, the sacrum, and neck.

Jane worked with a physical therapist in 2011 for shoulder pain of unknown origin and saw a podiatrist who fitted her with orthotics. From June 2012, Jane no longer needed taping. January 2013, she began to see a rolfer for a series of ten structural integration treatments. I recommended that she take a break from me during the series and focus on the benefits of the rolfing without interference from other bodywork. I also referred Jane to a chiropractor who weaned her off the orthotics. Jane deepened her yoga practice with pranayama (breathwork). She started juicing and improved her eating habits. She nurtured her spirituality, traveling to Brazil, Bolivia, Egypt, and Jerusalem.

I have been impressed by Jane's openness to try new modalities, many of which brought her immense relief and healing and some that didn't do much for her. I have encouraged Jane to listen to her body and now that she has made such progress on her healing journey, to decide how often and what sort of session with me she needs—based on her main complaint or goal (e.g., detox, reduce pain, lower stress). Jane was always gung ho to try things I learned in Germany. Likewise, she has introduced me to therapies and practitioners, and I am a better therapist for the alternatives I now can share with my clients, friends, and family.

Jane's health and well-being improved steadily. Her eyes became bright and clear; her skin tone and color improved; she lost thirty-five pounds; and her posture improved. She no longer suffers from debilitating headaches, sinus problems, and ankle and knee pain. Jane continues to strive toward optimal health. If and when she no longer needs my work, I will consider that a resounding success. But there will always be a connection between us, having worked together for so many years.

Madge Lockwood, LMT, is a 1998 graduate of the Chicago School of Massage Therapy (now known as Cortiva Institute), where she was a faculty member and a professional therapist 2002–2005. Madge has over twelve hundred hours of training in massage therapy and bodywork. She taught manual lymph drainage for the Soma Institute's Master Clinical Massage Therapy Diploma Program 2009–2011. Madge is currently a manual lymph drainage and oncology massage provider for Heartwood Foundation's Women and Cancer Program, which provides free supportive services to low-income women with cancer in the greater Chicagoland area.

lymphaticmassageworks.com

27

Tiffany Traynor and Brady Singleton
Our Daughter Is an Angel

As parents we fight for our children. We sacrifice ourselves and put our children first—no matter what the condition of their health is. Having two children fifty weeks apart, Brady and I learned to just go with the flow. When your child gets diagnosed with an illness, you measure the medications, rearrange your schedule, and make your child's life the priority. That is exactly what we did for our youngest daughter, Lana.

Brady and I met June 2008 while deployed to Iraq, and in November 2009, we had our first precious baby girl, Hailey. Three months later I was pregnant again, and so we decided to get out of the Army. We moved to Chicago so Brady could go to college. He would get up before the sun and not come home till about 10 p.m., also working to provide for our little family. He's the hardest working man I know.

Family news in September 2010 brought us to Bluffton, Indiana, and Brady left college. In November 2010, two weeks before Hailey turned one, our second precious baby girl, Lana, was born. My mom and my youngest brother moved to Indiana to help with the girls as I enrolled at Ivy Tech Community College of Indiana for a human services degree and Brady worked.

When Lana was eleven months old, I took her to the pediatrician because she had dark urine. He gave us antibiotics for a yeast infection and sent us home. A week later, my mom took Lana back to the doctor while I was in class. He sent them to the local ER, Bluffton Regional Hospital, and I rushed to meet them. My heart was pounding, and my thoughts were racing.

Lana's blood pressure kept testing dangerously high. The doctor sent us right away to Riley Hospital for Children in Indianapolis, two hours away, to confirm the results and get more blood work. Lana's numbers were right, and we were lucky she didn't have a stroke. Lana was admitted on the renal (kidney) floor and was scheduled for a biopsy in the morning. We knew it was something serious, but Brady and I tried to stay calm for Lana.

After about a week, we were told that Lana had "Diffuse Mesangial Hypercellularity," fancy words for her kidneys weren't working right and she was urinating out protein. She also had high cholesterol, high triglyceride levels, low blood protein levels, and swelling. The doctor put Lana on steroids and a low-sodium diet. We were to test her urine and blood pressure daily from home. Whatever it took, we were going to do.

We were back to Riley in January, thankful we had made it through the holidays. Lana had started to fill with water again, had dark urine, and was eating less. She had albumin treatments through a "central line" (two tubes coming out of her chest) at Riley and then as an outpatient at Bluffton Regional. During the four-hour treatments, Hailey wanted to run everywhere, while Lana wanted to run but couldn't because she was hooked up to an IV pole. All the while, I was trying to do my homework for Ivy Tech.

The treatments stopped working just like the medications had. Our next stay at Riley lasted almost a month. When admitted, Lana was so swollen with fluid and in so much pain, she barely ate or drank. The doctors pulled off eight pounds of fluids and then decided to take more drastic measures. They placed a dialysis catheter and a "G-tube" (a gastrostomy tube for nutrition and medication) in Lana's stomach. During the surgery, Lana needed a blood transfusion. She looked so tiny. All I wanted to do was hold our daughter, but I couldn't because she was covered in tubes. Brady and I would take turns, for my classes in Fort Wayne and his work in Bluffton. Our oldest stayed with my mom and would come down to Riley on the weekends. Other relatives visited, too. Several people pulled together and held fundraisers for Lana's medical expenses. When people say it takes a village to raise children, they're right. Without an excellent support system, we wouldn't have gotten through any of this.

To be able to take Lana home and do the full ten hours on the dialysis and nutritional feeding machines, Brady and I had been training on a doll. We re-taught Lana to crawl, walk, and eat. She had regular physical therapy, occupational therapy, music therapy, and a playgroup on the renal floor, and picked up on everything quickly.

March 2012, at sixteen months old, Lana returned home a whole new person—just like any other child on the playground. She would run as fast as her little legs would take her, and her laugh was contagious. If her shirt came up showing her tubes, people asked and always said, "Oh I couldn't even tell she was sick."

Hailey and Lana were inseparable; they even held hands in the car. They were the best of friends and had their own little language. When Hailey had dance class, Lana danced on the sideline. Lana loved books and was always bringing me books to read. A couple of times I caught her "reading" the phonebook. The girls would sing songs from *Daniel Tiger's Neighborhood*, one of Lana's favorite TV shows.

Other times, it was like having a newborn. We'd get up at night to fix her line, wash her down and change her bed when she threw up, and call the help line when we couldn't figure out how to stop the machine's beeping. At times, it was overwhelming, but Brady and I worked as a team. Sometimes Hailey even helped by bringing us the dialysis bags. We had a routine, and things were going well. I even managed to maintain membership in the Ivy Tech Honor Society and finished my associates' degree in May 2013. Lana was progressing nicely to the stage necessary for the transplant. Brady's mom was a donor match.

Finally, Lana was going to get a new kidney and be normal—able to take a bath and play in the water. We'd be able to travel without packing a box of medical gear. We were looking forward to the little things that some people take for granted. During the three preparatory rounds of "plasmapheresis" (a process of plasma exchange), Lana and I played and sang and cuddled. The day of Lana's transplant we were all so excited and celebrated and took pictures. We strolled down to see Brady's mom before her prep work. As Lana was being taken back for her surgery, she sang "Grownups Come Back" from *Daniel Tiger's Neighborhood*. With tears rolling down my face, I reassured her that we would see her in a little bit. Watching Lana get wheeled away was always hard for me. I want to be there and hold her hand when she's scared. But I couldn't. All I could do was wait in the waiting room.

In the recovery room, Lana looked so small. She was very lethargic and asked for "Mommy" (she could already see her daddy). I went to her side and held her hand. She kept asking for water, and the doctor kept saying not to give her anything except to rub ice chips on her lips. That night, we slept in her room. Suddenly I woke up to a bloodcurdling scream. I assumed Lana had had a bad dream. I spoke softly in her ear and went to lie back down. Suddenly bells and alarms on her machines rang. Nurses and staff were running in, trying to figure out what was going wrong and giving her air and CPR. Lana wasn't responding. Brady and I just stood there frozen. They took Lana to ICU for tests. My stomach sank. The rest of the day, doctors ran tests. The more tests they ran, the worse things looked.

Brady and I continued to sit and stare at our daughter, and to pray she would open her eyes. The doctor told me Lana had no brain function, that her brain was gone. Not believing her or not wanting to believe her, I insisted on seeing the brain scan. The doctor warned me it would be hard, but I wanted to see it for myself. There was nothing but a big black spot where Lana's brain should have been. We started calling close friends and family.

At 7 p.m., the doctors called us into the room. They all stood there looking at us. We knew what they were going to say, but nobody wanted to speak. Finally, one of them said those unforgettable words:

"She has left us." Brady almost fell to the floor. It was February 20, 2014. The flood of pain at that moment is indescribable. The pain is so deep and hurts so much, it's almost as if you feel your heart breaking. After we got ourselves back together, we let everyone there say good-bye. We brought Hailey in last, right as we had them stop the machines. Hailey gave her sister one last hug and kiss. Hailey will never forget how Lana had purple lips, and purple was her sister's favorite color. We got one last family picture as we sat holding Lana not wanting to let her go.

You would not believe the number of people who showed up at Lana's funeral. In three short years, Lana had touched many people. She was always just so happy and full of life—all smiles all the time. When Lana walked into any room, people smiled. They just loved her. Lana's death reminded people to love on their own children a little more and be thankful for what they have.

For a while, I went inside myself. I felt guilty, like I hadn't done enough. I was angry at God. How could he take away someone with such a kind heart so soon and who had so much to still teach us? I was heartbroken. We lost our baby girl. Someone suggested *Heaven is for Real: A Little Boy's Astounding Story of His Trip to Heaven and Back.* The book just made me even angrier at God. Why does this little boy (who was the same age as my daughter) get to live but not my daughter? What made this little boy so special? Did we not yell at God loud enough? Did we not pray hard enough?

The autopsy results were inconclusive. Because of what happened to our daughter, the hospital changed its procedures for handling transplant patients. Any child who has a transplant would be taken straight to ICU to be monitored more closely. Lana's thirst (when we were told not to give her water but only to rub ice chips on her lips) could have been a sign that something was wrong. Or something could have triggered an alarm before her bloodcurdling scream. Our hope is that no other parents will have to experience the high of their child finally being normal just to have it all ripped away because something went wrong and no one fully knowing just what that was.

Many people have asked how I stay so strong and keep going. The answer is simple. I still have another child who wakes me up every morning and needs me. Hailey would ask, "Why didn't God take me, too?" I said, "God knew I couldn't handle him taking both of you." Two years later, she still asks questions from time to time and gets very lonely missing her best friend.

I went through a phase of wanting another baby or to adopt a child. But when I thought about what I wanted in that child, I described my baby Lana. If I saw a baby girl, I would cry. It's still hard to be around baby girls. If parents scolded a child, I had an urge to tell them that you never know what tomorrow will bring and your child may not be here. Sometimes I just sat and cried or hugged something that used to be Lana's. I wanted to feel her again.

Nothing and no one can fill that empty space in our hearts. We just have to take life one day at a time, find a new normal, and live knowing the pain will never fully go away. I guess the trick is not to rush grief. Our society has a timeline for grief, but who cares really what others think? You have to do things when you're ready to do them, whether it is moving your loved one's stuff or talking about everything.

Talking about Lana helps me not cry as much. Now I can share memories of Lana and even laugh. For her birthday and on her death date, we have a dinner and send her lanterns or balloons. Holidays, too, are hard. We try to surround ourselves with people who miss Lana just as much as we do. Sometimes we turn on a small light that looks like a candle made with flowers from her funeral. Our memory of Lana will never go away because we have constant reminders all around our house and wear bracelets that say: "Lana Rose forever in our hearts."

Tiffany Traynor and Brady Singleton, veterans of the United States Army, live with their daughter, Hailey, in Bluffton, Indiana. Brady is an automotive technician/service writer at a local shop. Tiffany is a stay-at-home mom.

28

Jane Borden

The Messenger Bag of Happiness

A couple of years ago, I was a real jerk. I'd sit idly while my boyfriend, Nathan, did everything: the cooking, the cleaning, the shopping, and the laundry. I wouldn't enter a room or vehicle unless he opened the door first. Nathan even had to tip the glass to my lips for me to sip. Sometimes I made my friends and family perform these functions, too—and after all they did, I never sent a single thank-you note.

But when I say "jerk," I don't mean I was being rude or selfish. I mean the other definition of "jerk": a fool. I was a fool. My boyfriend was acting out of necessity, not chivalry. I'd contracted acute bilateral tendinitis, aka matchsticks that combusted in both shoulders whenever I used my hands. Fortunately, I could flush toilets with my toes, or Nathan would've had to follow me in there, too.

After six years as a magazine editor, squeezing seven days of work into five, I'd become keyboard efficient. Unfortunately, I wasn't keyboard correct. Eventually, my arm muscles, along with the inflamed tendons connecting them to my shoulder joints, long abused by millions of ergonomically unsound strokes, went on strike. If only we could have sat down for a talk first! But, then, I probably would've just made them transcribe it all.

I had no idea how self-sufficient I was, how much I did for myself, until suddenly I was useless. I couldn't carry or bear weight, or apply any pressure. I couldn't even use silverware. I subsisted on toddler snacks, soft food, and finger food (read: baby carrots, hummus, and sliced, whole wheat bread)—all of which had to be procured and carried home by someone else. Once, a pal came over with the express purpose of opening my mail. I had him rip individual articles out of the magazines so I'd have something to read in bed.

The orthopedist ordered me to rest the muscles and tendons, use them as little as possible, which was like, no duh: every time I did, tiny hillbillies lit bonfires in my rotator cuffs. So there I was, even if by accident, adhering to an archaic code of chivalry. I used to be the girl by the elevator, emphatically replying to the men, "No, no, after you." Now I was the girl sitting across the restaurant table from the other girl, who nudged her boyfriend and said, "You never cut my food for me!"

I hated it. Waiting in front of a heavy door until someone passed whom I could ask for help. So badly I wanted to grab the handle and pull. It's such a small and simple action. And after about a week of resting, once I had healed a bit, I knew that I could open doors without pain. But it would come at the cost of other actions, like brushing my teeth. The more I healed, the more motions I could perform in a day without overexerting myself. But if I exceeded my allotment, the next day's batch would be smaller and also full of hillbillies with torches. Since the pain was not always immediate and crept up on me, I had to estimate how much and for how long I could safely use my arms without setting back my recovery. I began to see tickets attached to the mundane actions of daily life, each bearing a different number: 3 to cut a piece of paper, 22 to chop a tomato, and 2,009 to slice a ball with a tennis racket. But, of course, I've never played tennis. At least now I have an excuse.

Still, my plan was working. I focused on incremental gains, and I began to heal. That is, until I re-injured myself. A doctor in Brighton Beach, whom my insurance company made me see, told me to return to work full time. I did and the next day, my tendinitis was worse than it had been initially. But slowly—this time it took about a month—I was beginning to recover again. Until the re-re-injury: My physical therapist pushed me too hard with the elastic bands, or as I now call them, elastic *ssholes.

Two weeks of total incapacitation grew into almost a year. Back and forth, up and down, strong and weak. My physical ability, or lack thereof, led to wild fluctuations in my mental health. My psychological well-being was tied to, solely determined by, the pain or lack of pain in my shoulders and upper arms. When I woke pain-free, I felt elated, invincible, like I could move mountains or, you know, a small folding chair. But when every little action roused the hillbillies' fireworks, I grew hopeless.

And no one seemed to know what was actually wrong. The tendinitis diagnosis was clear, but the MRI showed only a small amount, nothing that could be causing the problems I experienced. "I don't understand," said the orthopedist, shaking his head and lifting his shoulders, "it's just a little tendinitis." I started seeing specialists: a neurologist, an allergist / immunologist, an acupuncturist, two more orthopedists. My case baffled them all.

I felt helpless, out of control—because that's what happens when you lose agency. You're rendered passive. And then it's easy for inertia to keep you still. This is why women started riding bicycles! All but me, of course—too much weight bearing on the shoulders.

My low point arrived with summer. The hillbillies had set up camp in my shoulders without sign of moving on. I woke up, put on flats because I couldn't tie shoelaces, and then reached for the doorknob to leave. But the sudden rise in humidity had swollen the front door shut. I knew that yanking it would set me back at least a day, maybe two—and that, as is the nature of doors, it would only need to be opened again tomorrow. I saw a cycle without escape. I was trapped in my apartment. So I collapsed to the floor and started bawling. If I'd thought clearly, I could've looped a belt around the knob and yanked it with my teeth. But all I could think were "nevers." I'll never pilot a sailboat again; I'll never paint a room in a future home; I may as well throw away my lacrosse stick; I'll never be able to travel alone. All of my fears vomited out of me, including the two I'd worked the hardest to ignore: I'll never write again and I'll never be able to carry my own child.

As a teenager, I promised myself that if I were ever paralyzed, told I'd never walk again, that I'd be the case you read about in the newspaper, the patient who proved everyone wrong through willpower. Yet it hadn't taken much, just "a little tendinitis," for me to completely give up.

I was so focused on the pain, I hadn't seen the more dangerous development: I'd totally abdicated control. I'd put my fate in the hands of doctors and therapists, when none could even pinpoint the problem. They never told me anything new, yet I kept making appointments. I'd shifted the power to heal me onto everyone else but me. Dependence breeds despondence. I declared, "If no one knows what's wrong, then only I can know what's right." I mean, that Brighton Beach doctor hadn't forced me to type. The physical therapist hadn't held a gun next to those @#%! elastic bands.

Next, I decided that if it was going to take years for me to heal, then I'd have to forget I was injured. And in order to do that, I had to become self-sufficient. Nathan never complained about helping me—he is now my husband, which is to say, I wouldn't let a guy like that go—but I no longer wanted his help. So we found a messenger bag I could strap around my waist. I wore it to the grocery store, slid items off of shelves until they fell into the open bag, waddled up to the checkout lane, hip-flipped the bag onto the counter, rolled the items out, and then let the cashier put everything back in.

I memorized which doors to which entrances were push instead of pull. I discovered the amazing tool God has given us in teeth. They unscrew plastic soda-bottle caps, flip stubborn light switches, turn deadbolt locks. And, here's a tip: If your sink fixtures are as difficult to twist as mine were, try turning on the bath faucet with your foot, and then, while it's on, filling every glass in the apartment with water; they'll be too heavy for you to carry, but that's why you keep straws around.

Even when the pain didn't ease, the depression did. And then, I began to forget. Slowly, I stopped thinking of myself as handicapped. A year and a half later, I'm happy to say that I no longer use my feet for any non-foot function—except to flush toilets (you really shouldn't touch those handles, especially not after my feet have). But I do still carry bags around my waist. I no longer think of it as a strange and an onerous adjustment, though. It's just how I live. The mind has an amazing capacity to adapt and forget.

Somewhere along the way, I even came to terms with the fact that I probably won't ever type again. I produced this article the way I do all of my writing (including most of my first book): with dictation software. It takes longer and the results are spotty, but, again, it's just the way I write now, nothing more or less. It's just the way it is. My life doesn't always look like it used to, but at least I accept it and I'm in control of it. Which leads me to believe that I have found the key to happiness. Self-sufficiency. Really, it's so simple that a two-year-old can tell you. "I want to do it myself." I hear my niece say it all the time. Sometimes, it's while I'm carrying her.

Jane Borden is a culture journalist and the author of *Cults Like US: How Doomsday Drives America* (One Signal, 2023) and *I Totally Meant to Do That* (Crown, 2011).
JaneBorden.com/journalism
Instagram.com/JaneBorden

A version of this article was previously published as "Still Life: How I Learned to Flush a Toilet with My Feet" in *O'Henry Magazine* (November 2012).

29

Lucette Doss

Can You Imagine?

I have been a devotee of the Blessed Virgin Maria [Mother Mary—Ed.] for many years and always wanted to visit Lourdes, France, the pilgrimage site dedicated to her, but raising three children and running a business alone after my husband died had kept me from going. And then one morning I woke up before 9 a.m. and knew I had to go to Lourdes. Now. I immediately phoned my travel agent and by the next day, all arrangements had been purchased for a ten-day stay. Can you imagine?

On the flight from Canada to France, I tripped over a man's outstretched leg in the aisle while walking to the bathroom. The fall resulted in a large bruise on my right breast. Little did I know this was Virgin Maria's first gift to me.

After returning home to Montreal, I visited the doctor who surprised me by recommending a mammogram. The results came back clear, but the doctor was still not satisfied and recommended a biopsy. When the biopsy also came back clear, she persisted that we do a third test. Two days before my sixty-fourth birthday, the doctor called to say I had stage III breast cancer and recommended an operation as soon as possible. Within just two weeks, on July 15, 2013, I had an operation to remove the tumor, which is considered pretty quick for Canada's medical system. My second divine gift.

September 10 has become an important day for me. It was that day in 2013 I began my chemotherapy. Throughout the challenges of losing my hair, being unable to move for many months, and losing my appetite, I stayed firm in my belief "this is nothing" because I knew the

Virgin Maria was with me. After all, if I had not spontaneously decided to go to Lourdes and had not fallen on the plane traveling there, I would not have gone to the doctor. And if I had not sought out a doctor who followed her instincts and would not give up, I most likely would be dead. The doctor said that if they had not found it when they did, the tumor most probably would have moved to my bones undetected and been fatal. I firmly believe the Virgin Maria, the saint I have held close to my heart for many years, guided me. She saved my life. Can you imagine?

The divine mother had another miraculous gift up her sleeve. After completing my chemotherapy in March 2014, I decided to return to Lourdes for the month of May, the month dedicated to the Virgin Maria, to give thanks for her help. Towards the end of my stay, a fellow hotel guest had spotted me and become my secret admirer. While I was checking out of our hotel, we finally met. Charles introduced himself and asked for my contact information and if he could call me when I returned to Canada. He was only in Lourdes for a few days, and our paths crossed right as I was departing for home. Can you imagine? One month later, coincidentally on my birthday, Charles called me and asked if he could come visit me September 10, my special day of healing. I was so happy. My third heavenly gift.

Charles, my new eighty-five-year-old friend, arrived in Montreal from his home in France and stayed with me for eighteen days. We traveled around Canada and were very, very happy. Like teenagers. He wrote the following poem for me, his "amitia" (friend for life), which he says is better than love because this affection never dies. The poem was published in his *Poésies Naïves et Spontanées* [Naïve and spontaneous poems].

Je flânais, ce jour-là
rêvant au bord du Gave
à la joie, au bonheur
aux larmes, aux tristesses.
La grotte était tranquille
et la Vierge veillait.
Et j'aperçus, alors,
à l'ombre des platanes
une humble silhouette
un halo de lumière
brillant à ses côtés.
Nos regards se croisèrent
et nous nous reconnûmes.
Comme deux vieux amis
qui se croyaient perdus.
Et depuis ce jour-là
nos vies sont apaisées,
le ciel plus lumineux
et le bonheur tranquille.
Mais, Lucette,
Pourriez-vous m'oublier
et qui suis-je!

I strolled, that day
dreaming of the River Gave
the joy, happiness,
tears and sadness.
The cave was quiet
and the Virgin watched.
And reflected, then,
in the shade of the large trees
a humble figure
a brilliant light
by her side.
Our eyes met
and we recognized each other.
Like two old friends
who believed lost.
And since that day
our lives are peaceful,
the sky brighter
and the happiness quiet.
But, Lucette
can you forget me
and who I am!

Lourdes
ce mois de Mai
de l'An de Grâce
2014
(Charles Leuret)

Lourdes
May
2014
(Charles Leuret)

September 10 is my day of miraculous healing—body and soul. It is the day I began cleansing my body of a cancer and the day I acquired an amitia. Just imagine. It all started with receiving and following the nudge to go to Lourdes, and trusting in Virgin Maria to deliver miracles. It's fantastic. I am so very, very happy.

Lucette Doss lives in Montreal, Canada, and has three children with her husband Ezaat Doss, now deceased. She also has three grandchildren. Lucette enjoys cooking and traveling. Her generosity, joie de vivre, strength, and faith continue to guide her every step in life.

30

Nancy M. Turcich

A Walking Miracle

With fall colors popping all over campus, I yearned to absorb some of the natural beauty surrounding Southern Illinois. October 1982, I was nineteen years old and a college sophomore. I gathered some friends and headed to Little Grand Canyon, part of the Shawnee National Forest in Simpson. We weren't hikers or climbers, just kids out for a day in nature.

As the canyon cooled, I followed my friend Michael up to the top of a cliff towards the shining sun. In a short time, we were hailed by our companions. While making our descent, I chose a rocky surface—an old riverbed that seemed to be the most direct and quickest route to our friends waiting in the canyon. What appeared to be a continuous path dropped forty feet. And so did I. Landing on my posterior, a boulder crushed three vertebrae in my upper spine while another rock snapped my right wrist. Paralysis rapidly set in.

A miracle is an event that takes place when logic and practicality says it can't. I had not thought of my healing as miraculous, though due to the distance that I fell and the severity of my injury, I was told that I was a miracle. It took about eight years for me to feel the miracle. My healing involved hard work and daily dedication. The true miracle was the response of my nervous system to the spinal injury. I can't explain why my nervous system responded, but I'm grateful it did. Doctors told me that patients with less injury were not walking. Months and lots of gumption later, I was walking and performing every physical motion.

According to the allopathic medical world, following a spinal fusion, a body cast, a brace, and then freedom from all apparatus, within six months I could move; therefore, I was healed. With a monster-like gait, nearly nonexistent balance, and constant muscle spasms, my body was less than my own. But I was a "miracle;" consequently, I was "OK" in the eyes of the mainstream medical world. My true healing took much longer—years, even decades.

In 1985, I entered the New Mexico School of Natural Therapeutics (NMSNT) in Albuquerque to become a Natural Therapeutic Specialist, which included massage and Polarity Therapy. Polarity Therapy is an Eastern-based energy therapy, whereas the better-known Swedish massage is based on the venous system. Polarity can be done while the client is dressed or undressed; Swedish is done while the client is unclothed and applies oil. Polarity is based on the energetic principles of attraction, repulsion, and neutrality and follows the five elements, the chakras, the triads, and the yin and the yang. Swedish works on the physical structure, pushing blood to the heart to flush the muscles.

The NMSNT program jumpstarted my healing. After intense poking and prodding during my initial recovery, gentle restorative touch calmed my nervous system and eased my musculature. Bodywork and body awareness have taken me far into my healing and knowing myself. Awareness is key, allowing me to recognize when I am in balance or out of balance, at one with myself or separate. I monitor my life physically, energetically, mentally, emotionally, and spiritually. Each of these realms influences my behavior. If these systems are running smoothly, my body will calm and relax or fire up my engines—as needed. I also rest and eat well.

I used to be frustrated, angry, and confused. Since my natural therapeutic training, I have discovered ways to adapt and find more of me: to be at peace, to recognize the beauty that surrounds me, to love life, to experience joy readily, to just be. That has been my greatest gift. I call it "resourcing" because it allows me to find myself again. In so doing, I show others how to find their way, which is the most positive and effective outcome of my work.

My healing partners have come in many shapes and sizes. When I started my school program at NMSNT, natural healing was foreign to me. Loving touch versus invasive touch was a welcome change, allowing my body to respond instead of react to outside influences. During hands-on training sessions, classmates let my hypersensitive body jump, shake, rattle, and roll. Although some were frightened, most were intrigued by my unique nervous system. My body was an excellent teacher and has been my greatest healing partner. From head to toe, wise beyond measure, it has taught me more about how to be with another person than any healing method or instruction.

Every time I required a therapist or healer, I found the perfect match. I listened to what he or she had to share and I learned what worked for me. It wasn't about him or her or a skill set; it was about my body and how I responded to the skills. On a regular basis, I received bodywork to tune into my body through the touch of others. This was important because paralysis had erased some of my sensations. My partner's ability to hold space and permit my body the opportunity to do what it needed to do was crucial. Trusting that my body and my spirit were in ultimate charge, I was able to let go and follow the therapist's lead.

To this day, I tell others to trust yourself and your system. If you need to rest, rest. If you need touch, get touch. If you need a friendly ear, find someone to listen. Be kind to yourself. Every one of us has the answers within ourselves. We tend to disregard our instincts and seek answers elsewhere. Although I believe others can and do help, they are simply sounding boards and guides. Deep down inside, we each know what we need to do and be in this world. A good place to start is to change what is within your power and to strive to decrease the enormity of what feels out of your control. Accept where you are today and if that's impossible, try again tomorrow.

Healing may not take place when you want it, but it is always within you. When we are out of balance, we say we are unhealthy or sick. The system has gone into an imbalanced state but there is also balance within. If we hit our head, are we unwell? Yes and no. The body will do what it needs to do to find balance again. Health is always there. It changes, but it is there. Let go of time constraints. Take a step toward your goal, and then another step. It takes persistence and hard work. People always told me to thank God for my healing, but I felt I deserved credit for all that I did to get there. Hope is good, but it's not everything.

Life brings many challenges. Knowing we are not alone somehow makes it possible to go on, to fight the fight. When I discover kinder spirits, I am uplifted. Stories matter; it's that simple. People read others' stories and recognize they are not alone. I plan to continue to help people find their way, to provide one-on-one healing programs, to speak publicly, to teach Polarity and Trauma Therapy, and to go where I am needed and wanted.

Nancy M. Turcich began her training at the New Mexico School of Natural Therapeutics (NMSNT) and has been a therapist since 1986. She is a Natural Therapeutic Specialist (NTS), a Board Certified Polarity Practitioner (BCPP), and a Registered Polarity Practitioner. Nancy developed the *Find Your Way Program* (online and in-person) to assist others in their healing. She is also an educational speaker and the author of *Finding My Way from Paralysis to a Rich, Full Life* (Prescott, AZ: Bez Publications, 2009) and *One of Eight: My Perspective on our Brother's Suicide* (Prescott, AZ: Bez Publications, 2005). She is based in Prescott, Arizona.

naturalmassagetherapy.com

31

Frank Baldassare

The Perfect Storm

One day, my friend and I were driving in the car when she told me the story of what her four-year-old granddaughter had said to her. Children can be brutally honest, and this little tyke was no different.

"What's wrong, Grandma?" she asked, "You seem to be in a bad mood."

My friend responded, "It has nothing to do with you, Sweetie. Grandma's just not in a good mood today."

"Grandma, pull the plug on that!" she demanded.

My friend and I burst out laughing. This wise four-year-old reminded me of one of the most important lessons I learned from my illness and subsequent healing: we are our thoughts. Our thoughts become our actions and affect our emotions and thereby, our health. Visualizing good things brings about positive results. When you find yourself in a negative place, "Pull the plug on that."

Despite six years of my chronic sickness, from November 2001, the healing process was grounded upon my intense drive to control the disease. Diet, laughter, exercise, a focus on reconnecting my body, mind, and spirit, and the occasional "pulling of the plug" on negative thoughts were keys to rediscover harmony and restore balance in my life.

A healthy lifestyle has always been a major pursuit and a career interest of mine. Born and bred in New York State, I moved to New York City to model and study acting and I also waited tables. I then taught fitness and became the Head of Fitness for Club Med in St. Lucia. Returning to Manhattan, I earned my degree from the Swedish Institute College of Health and Science in 1993. I worked in the health and wellness field as a massage therapist in New York. In

1998, I was nominated as the "Best Massage Therapist in the Business" by Vogue magazine.

Then suddenly in 2002, at age forty, my life changed dramatically. One night, I went to bed and the next morning, I woke up ill. Given my healthy orientation and professional commitments, I was even more shocked. I had trouble with my eyes. I had pains in my bones, my joints, and the nerves in my legs. Although the doctor told me my blood work was normal, I dropped twenty-four pounds in five weeks.

After many trips to numerous specialists, in February 2002, I went back to the gastroenterologist Karim S., who had helped me with a parasitic infection contracted in my twenties while working for Club Med in the Caribbean. I had never had allergies or been prone to digestive disorders or even had a sensitive stomach.

I brought all of my medical records, none of which Dr. S. needed. He took one look at me and asked, "Why hasn't anyone checked you for Celiac Disease?" I had never heard of Celiac Disease, but Dr. S. was right. My tests came back positive. I had Celiac Disease, an autoimmune disease triggered by gluten. The doctor informed me that there is no cure, and the treatment is strict adherence to a gluten-free diet.

The son of a military man, I followed a gluten-free diet like a disciplined marine for eight months without any positive results. So I saw more doctors. One said I was depressed and prescribed anti-depression medication. I told him, "I'm not depressed, I'm sick." Another doctor wanted to put me on prednisone, a potent corticosteroid and immunosuppressant used to treat inflammation.

Licensed in Shiatsu and having studied Chinese medicine at the Swedish Institute and with others post-graduation, I have always leaned more towards Oriental practices with my clients' healing processes and for my own self-care. Thus, I refused the doctor's advice to take the drugs they prescribed.

Instead, in 2004, I went to Barnes & Noble and located every book on the immune system and contacted each author. I followed the protocol of Ken Bock (*The Road to Immunity: How to Survive and Thrive in a Toxic World*, 1997), a heavy-duty vitamin and mineral program to replace the nutrients my body was unable to absorb from the food I ate due to my intestinal damage from Celiac Disease. Even as we are fighting for a correct diagnosis, we are prone to symptoms from complications that further mask an accurate diagnosis. I had bone and skin problems, nerve damage and nerve pain, and chronic fatigue.

One day, I realized that laughter had left my life completely. In that moment, I knew I was being called to action. Sometimes God nudges us into action, and in this case, he had knocked me flat on my face. Lying on Dr. S.'s table as he painfully pressed my abdomen, I announced, "You know I'm going to make sense of this, right? There's something for me to do here."

I decided to make some major changes in my life and to make my health my number one priority. At the time, I owned a record label for dance and relaxation music for the spa industry, and I assigned the business over to my partner and used my investment to support my new mission. I walked my dogs daily through Central Park in Manhattan. I began weekly massage treatments. I started to observe my sickness from an Eastern healing perspective and reviewed the facts. My body had been attacking itself, so what was around me when I started to get sick? I had grown tired of the music business, and I was surrounded by toxic personal relationships. These factors were the perfect storm for illness.

I decided to clear the deck and use my professional experience in massage therapy and caring for people to help show others a way to make positive changes in their lives. One day in 2003, I was sitting at home watching Food Network. It hit me that these cooking shows often ignore the issue of food intolerance and allergies. After giving it some thought, I phoned a friend who is a cameraman for Discovery Channel and told him my idea for a cooking show called The Missing Ingredient®. That ingredient was gluten. The show, I explained, would teach an audience how to adjust recipes for certain dieting requirements.

A Food Network executive who I pitched the show to loved the idea, but concluded the market was not large enough for such a show. In 2003, I put the show on the Internet for free at themissingingredienttv. com. I was motivated by several reasons. Friends had modern, well-equipped kitchens that they used for storage instead of for cooking and ate out constantly. I want to get people back in the kitchens because my friends have admitted to feeling better when I cook for them. I also want to bring families together. Why not use Celiac Disease or food allergies as the perfect excuse for bringing families around the table to eat? Turn a negative into a positive.

Since the show has been on the Internet, I have received many positive reviews. From 2008, I have made several appearances on Martha Stewart Living. Much of my work now involves speaking to large groups about my experience. For the past three years, I have been a speaker at the annual Education Conference & Food Faire sponsored by the Celiac Disease Foundation. I have a passion for helping people understand the impact of food on their health. We have grown up in the era of prepared foods, and the average person's knowledge about what they are putting into their body is slim to none.

During my six years of sickness, I did not feel whole. My body, spirit, and mind were divided and refused to work together. Nonetheless, I felt spurred on by something, and I attribute that to God. I felt that this illness took my prior experience in entertainment, restaurants, health, and massage therapy, and put it all together. It seemed as if everything I had done in my life had been building to this.

My illness made me aware that miracles happen every day. It also has made me grateful for the small things and the ordinary, day-to-day activities. I found that sometimes it's crucial during the healing process to reevaluate what you're around and whom you're around. And don't forget that there's a little fight in all of us. As my grandfather used to say, "We come into this world kicking and screaming, and we leave the same way." That's why we should keep plugging along, because something magical could always happen. Tomorrow could be the day you're waiting for.

Frank Baldassare of North Salem, New York, is a leading figure in the gluten-free and allergy-friendly cooking movement. He is the creator and host of the cooking show The Missing Ingredient® and a frequent speaker at industry conferences. Frank is the founder and CEO of the lifestyle brand Cody Boy Entertainment ("the home of healthy entertainment"), which specializes in original, relevant health and wellness programs, children's literary properties, music, personal care products, and food services. A graduate of the Swedish Institute College of Health and Science in New York City, Frank has over three decades of experience in the health and wellness field. His journey began when he struggled with debilitating symptoms of Celiac Disease and successfully restored his health.

themissingingredienttv.com/wp-content/uploads/2011/01/Frank_Baldassare_full_bio1.pdf

codyboyentertainment.com

Epilogue
Back to School

Standing in gratitude before Heavenly Team Jane, I review the changes since my first internship. I am healthier, happier, and more open to new ideas and healing treatments. I have embraced my role as an explorer. I have grown in many ways. I smile because I like who I have become. I know there is more to learn and more work to do. I cheerfully switch gears to the future and re-enroll as an apprentice to become Jane the Inspirer. I review my fourteen tools and identify those experiences that may be useful on my upcoming adventure. I stop myself from wondering what the future holds. I shrug. I know firsthand the easy way is to use my past lessons as a guiding light and to follow my intuition as I take one step at a time. I feel like I did as Jane the Explorer. Excited and uncertain. I have more confidence now, and I know my next journey will be another ride of a lifetime.

Recently, I heard the following Native American story "Tale of Two Wolves" and thought it pretty much sums up my you heal you journey thus far.

One evening, an elderly Cherokee Brave told his grandson about a battle that goes on inside people. He said, "My son, the battle is between two 'wolves' inside us all. One is evil. It is anger, envy, jealousy, sorrow, regret, greed, arrogance, self-pity, guilt, resentment, inferiority, lies, false pride, superiority, and ego. The other is good. It is joy, peace, love, hope, serenity, humility, kindness, benevolence, empathy, generosity, truth, compassion, and faith." The grandson thought about it for a minute, and then asked, "Which wolf wins?" The old Cherokee simply replied, "The one that you feed." (Author unknown.)

Early in my life, I fed the evil wolf. Once I became Jane the Apprentice, I began feeding the good wolf, and my life shifted for the better. I ignored negative thoughts in my head (the evil wolf) and focused on the positive and inspirational thoughts from Heavenly Team Jane (the good wolf). The choice was always mine to make. It still is. I choose to keep this strategy in the forefront of my mind going forward. Old habits have a way of popping back up, and I want to stay focused on my good wolf.

After hearing "Tale of Two Wolves," I had flashbacks of trips to Scotland where I had encountered wolves. In northern Scotland, their howls late at night woke me up and gave me the creeps. On the Isle of Skye, I dreamed that wolves were pacing outside my bedroom door, guarding it (and thus, protecting me). Really. What are the odds? Was Heavenly Team Jane starting to drip the idea on me about the two wolves within?

I was feeding the good wolf when I took as my motto, "It's not what happens to you, but how you react." It helped me focus on the hope of what could come versus fretting over what had happened. This discipline helped me emerge into a modern day warrior, someone who lovingly protects and rescues herself. When negative opinions try to keep me in the past, I am able to stand in my power by responding, "It doesn't matter. It's what I do today that matters. And I am going to make something good come from these past experiences." After a while, the negative voices quit picking on me as much.

To some people, my steps to heal myself may make no sense. That is OK. In fact, it is perfect. It only needs to make sense to me. I grow more confident as I stand my ground and not let persuasive voices direct my behavior. I stay assured by reading accounts of other modern day warriors.

Me healing me is a work-in-progress. Although I expected to feel better after doing my part by creating my unique healing formula, I was surprised when additional healing came from writing my story for *You Heal You*. It was necessary to suppress certain emotions while in survival mode to contain my despair and stave off self-pity—both energy drains. When I moved into recovery mode, these blocked feelings were holding me back, something I had not anticipated. Reliving my experiences through writing my story opened old, hidden wounds, enabling me to heal further. Freedom! Storytellers who participated in *You Heal You* expressed similar thoughts. We wanted to share our journeys to inspire others, and were surprised when the writing, editing, and refining process further advanced our healing. I now leave room for unexpected wonders in my unique healing formula and new steps on my stairway to joy.

All my struggles, doubts, and agonies got me to where I am today. Every labor was worth it. I was not like the butterfly, who was spared the effort of emerging naturally from its cocoon and thus, was unable to fly. (Chapter 12, The Wings of a Prayer) Thankfully, Heavenly Team Jane did not step in and do my work like the little boy in the butterfly story. Instead, my team inspired me to keep going. "This is only a pit stop along the journey, Jane." My difficulties propelled me upward to my next and ongoing apprenticeship as Jane the Inspirer.

If given the chance to turn back the clock thirty years and walk the same path knowing the challenges ahead, I would choose to do it again. Absolutely. Because of the joy I picked up along the way and the realization of the power I had to heal myself. The only thing I would change is having a book like *You Heal You* to inspire me when I was fearful, anxious, in pain, and having trouble hearing Heavenly Team Jane. I looked and couldn't find one, and that's one of the reasons I wrote *You Heal You*.

My stairway to joy is like peeling an onion. The more layers I peel away, the more layers I see. Just like being Heavenly Team Jane's intern again. I finished one apprenticeship, and another one showed up. I adopted the circle and the triangle as the YouHealYou™ icon to represent this ongoing (the circle) change (a triangle). I chose "inspire, redirect, heal" as my tagline to remind me and others that you heal you is a process. As I continue to peel away layers, I become more skillful at working through them. My life gets easier and definitely more joyful. My goal is to earn my wings, like the angel Clarence in *A Wonderful Life*.

My healing mission is not done yet. I will be adding new steps to my stairway to joy. And I fully expect Heavenly Team Jane has several more internships for me. I don't know what the future holds, but I do know when my heavenly squad is involved it is quite the adventure. A rush of excitement. Stay tuned for this and other modern day warriors' latest you heal you adventures in future books as we continue to rescue ourselves.

Jane's Healing Mission Continues

(2020–)

Jane G. Doyle

How I Thrived during the COVID-19 Pandemic

The citywide order for shelter-in-place for COVID-19 illness[1] had been in force less than twenty-four hours. March 19, 2020, my inward trek began. At home in Chicago, I logged onto Facebook and lay down under my crystal healing bed, a color light therapy treatment using Vogel crystals.[2] My favorite healing center in Brazil, Casa de Dom Inacio de Loyola (known as "The Casa") was livestreaming every day at noon. This house of love where the medicine is love, was spreading love currents worldwide. For the next eighty minutes, we shared prayers, silent contemplation, inspiration, and the high vibrational energy from this center of miracles. We closed with a community prayer.

The next day, I logged on again, and then at least six times a week for the next year. The Casa's dedication to humanity, my commitment to regular participation, our collective power, and the energy from the Casa transformed me for the good. Heck, even my diet started to change. During this Jane time, I began to see unresolved fears and stuck emotional traumas, and how much power I gave away to mindless groupthink instead of active critical thinking. I witnessed myself healing in ways I thought not possible (my definition of a "miracle," chapter 7). It was my first of three life turning points during the global rampage of the COVID-19 pandemic.

---

1. Public Health Order No. 2020-1: Shelter in Place for COVID-19 Illness, issued and effective March 18, 2020, Order of the Commissioner of Health of the City of Chicago, https://www.chicago.gov/city/en/sites/covid-19/home/health-orders.html

2. Ababridges, https://tinyurl.com/2p8m5et3

My second life turning point was inspired by Lorie Ladd, a spiritual thought leader.

The third life turning point was meeting Wise Jane, a new member of Heavenly Team Jane (HTJ), my divine advisors.

From Jane the Apprentice (Scotland, 2002–2008) to Jane the Explorer (Brazil, 2009–2012) to Jane the Inspirer (America, 2013–), I now embarked on an armchair adventure With Wise Jane (Inner World, 2020–). My new stage of discovery is shaping up to be just as spectacular as the others.

***

When Chicago started a series of restrictions and closures in mid-March 2020, I went into survival mode. I intuitively relied on my fourteen tools (each its own chapter) that I had established in *You Heal You* (2016), but now, were on steroids as maintenance lifelines. For example, chapter 8, Take Responsibility) evolved to Take Radical Responsibility and centered on setting firmer boundaries, especially regarding the fear surrounding the threat of the pandemic. Victimhood was out the door.

Before, when my debilitating illnesses of the prior decades overwhelmed me, "I broke it down to one hour at a time and even ten-minute increments. This discipline stopped me from feeling self-pity and desperation" (p. 18). Now with the pandemic, I was dealing with more than my own fears. I was saddled with the world's fears, too. I took life one day at a time, and now even one minute at a time. I remained focused on the day. I became a moment-to-moment girl.

Within a month of regular Casa love currents, I noticed my continual headaches started to disappear, a condition I previously thought not possible. A miracle! My daily chronic headaches, which had begun in the early 1980s, in my mid-twenties, never fully ceased, but by 2009, were no longer debilitating. (See chapters 1, 8, and 26.) I declared them healed when they were no longer 24/7, and manageable with over-the-counter medications. April 2020, the remaining headaches started to ease. The volume was turned down. The only thing that I had changed was the daily Casa livestream.

Six months later, I stopped taking all pain relievers, and even the memory of headaches was gone. A condition I had lived with all day, every day for over three decades was out of my energy field. Miraculous, especially considering this happened during the most stressful first month of the global crisis. My heavenly team of divine healing allies, was back to visually strutting its stuff.

Since I still went by el train into my downtown office, I invested in myself (Chapter 9) by creating a COVID-19 wellness plan. My physician checked my vital signs regularly, administered acupuncture as needed, and reviewed my immune-boosting protocol and supplements regimens. I kept my distance from others, wore a mask, did not travel or eat out, spent holidays alone, and made sure I got plenty of rest. Success! I remained healthy (Chapter 12, Me Healing Me).

I enjoyed Jane time. The regular prayer currents were keeping me sane in an increasingly insane world. Instead of focusing on the fear cloud building in the world, I stayed grounded in the power of prayer, hope, and miracles in a universe I was creating. I had a flashback to my Myers-Briggs Type indicator personality test results from the 1980s. I scored evenly between extraversion and introversion, and yet, I had been starving my introvert all those years with a supercharged active lifestyle. I even called the Casa a spa for my soul. But during the lockdown, I received full spa treatment. My at-home self-retreat was an unexpected gift and a wake-up call to the needs of my introvert self (Chapter 5, Listening to My Body). Despite indulging in solitude, I never felt alone. Probably because I was never really alone.

At the start of 2021, my divine healing allies showed up again. Work began on an old right ankle injury (see chapter 12), which had flared up unprovoked by a fall or twist. During a January snowstorm, I noticed that my ankle was swollen, and I could barely put weight on it. Within a day or two, I was severely limping. There was no clear diagnosis from the medical professionals. An arthritis flare-up? Anti-inflammatory medicine helped the swelling somewhat, but worked better on my allergic reaction to the cleaning supplies now being used in Chicago public transportation and my office building. Major win for allergies, but not for walking.

After receiving no clear diagnosis about my right ankle problems, I paused to regroup. It was then my reliable healing allies once again came forward. During the crystal bed sessions, I felt sensations in my right calf that spread until my whole right leg and hip felt numb. The tingling ceased right before the currents of love stopped. Hmm. What a coincidence.

Was my leg just falling asleep?

Or was the divine at work?

After each session, I walked better and the long-term ankle swelling was receding. Hmm.

My hunch was correct. HTJ was at it again. They make the most excellent healing partners (see chapter 10). I was reminded of my visit to St. Ninian's Cave in Scotland, where I learned miracles are on the other end of struggles if I pause and don't give up (Chapter 6).

I watched videos on self-healing techniques and miracles that people had sent me. Now I had time to devour them, which led to my second life turning point. Like the first, it was prompted by an act of kindness. Out of the blue, July 26, 2020, a friend sent me the video "See through the Fear Narratives | This Is Why You Are Here,"[3] by Lorie Ladd. A woman—Lorie—with long blond hair and a mic pinned to the lapel of her lilac jacket is sitting in a car on a sunny day. She tells us to reclaim our sovereignty by awakening the innate wisdom within. Three min-

---

3. Lorie Ladd, "See through the Fear Narratives | This Is Why You Are Here," July 21, 2020, video, 12:36, https://tinyurl.com/s69vcw4m.

utes into the video, she refers to "warriors of the light." I was hooked. I was captivated by Lorie's concepts and became Jane the Explorer again, this time into the inner reaches of me. Game on.

Lorie also talked about "your higher self." I didn't know who that is or what it might be. Until one day, I heard a whisper inside me. I just assumed it was HTJ. But, goodness gracious, she's different from the other members of my divine advisors. She feels like a part of me, instead of outside of me like my angels and other HTJ members.

She also communicates differently. I get one thought at a time. Her instructions are simple. I am reminded of playing the game Jane's Treasure Hunt (Chapter 14), where you solve one clue before you receive the next one and sometimes without knowing the treasure you are seeking. Her voice is quieter. She is more neutral—no good, bad, or ugly. When I disagree, she is nonjudgmental and pro-free will. Like a navigational system that does not question why you ignored the recommended route, but instead replies, "recalculating." No shame. No limits. I felt empowered, and most of all, I felt safe. This is not my ego. This is not my regular HTJ. This is miraculous.

I welcomed this new member to HTJ, whom I would later dub "Wise Jane." Her presence promoted my third life turning point. I had the perfect ally for this new adventure. Wise Jane is all about the now. (You'll recognize Chapter 2, Being in the Moment.) Not the past or future. The present. Wise Jane is a big proponent of divine timing, and hers was impeccable. She was exactly what I needed during a pandemic.

When I struggled with seeing the positive coming from the present world crisis, Wise Jane repeatedly said, "All is perfect." What was so perfect about this pandemic? When I calmed down, I understood she meant that everything happening to me was perfect. Not to others. She was laser focused on only me and helping me evolve. My biggest cheerleader. My life's monitor. My healing partner. My best friend. Wise Jane.

As in my original anthology *You Heal You* (2016), I realized how vital looking for the positive is for any recovery and a happy life. I needed to up my game to survive a frustrating lockdown and keep a serious virus at bay. It was time to revisit and understand chapter 4, Seeing the Good, on a deeper level. When anything positive happened to me, I wrote it down and taped it to my front door. I needed the daily reminder. Seeing this list grow, I kept hope alive and counterbalanced the tidal wave of fear. I began to realize the wisdom in her advice. Wise Jane.

Wise Jane nudged me to drill down on my fears of COVID-19 and remember the part fear had played during my three decades of undiagnosed, debilitating illnesses (see A Conversation with Jane G. Doyle). I learned how small anxieties can grow into emotional cancer. Mitigating these fears was essential for my recovery. They were clouding sound judgment and blocking my connection to HTJ, my best advisors. Had I slipped back into a fearful mode? Or was I using the pandemic as an opportunity to polish my fear blocking shield and not allow the contagious anxieties of others to affect me? My choice. Time to do something about it.

I read voraciously and watched videos of experts about the diagnosis and prevalence of and treatments for COVID-19 in mainstream media and on social media. Much was conflicting. Most was fearful. What and who do I believe? How was I to navigate through this labyrinth of information? Again, I referred to YHY (2016) and how I had successfully healed myself. I launched my own research using my intuition as a truth finder and set out to create a new unique healing formula (UHF) (Chapter 11) to keep me safe and sound. It was time for me to leave my comfort zone (Chapter 3). I had my marching orders: commit to a regular practice of love currents, follow my gut (Chapter 1), limit fear, build your immune system, search for the good, and turn off the news. I will hear what I need to hear when I need to hear it.

The anchor of my new UHF for unique Jane was to unplug from the chaos and become the objective observer. Clear-eyed decisions in uncommon times were called for. Staying present by taking one day at a time was the glue. By eliminating distractions, I gave myself time. Time to listen to me. Time to uncover another level of unresolved emotions and traumas. Time to rest my physical body. Time to feed my soul. Time to take care of myself.

June 2021, Chicago started to open up again. I emerged as the same empath I had always been, but a different, stronger warrior Jane. I flew back to the Brazilian Casa for another tsunami of love. Sixteen days of love loving love (Chapter 13, Singing My Joy).

***

I returned to my modern day warrior mindset to shield myself from catching this deadly virus. I had walked life-threatening, treacherous paths before. I knew what to do. I retraced my fourteen you heal you steps. It was easier the second time around. I carefully listened for HTJ, focused on the positive, outlawed fear and self-pity, educated myself, and ventured into new frontiers of wisdom.

I chose the world I wanted to live in. Despite how horrific and gut-wrenching the past twenty months of the pandemic, I created a safe haven. I learned how media can be a drug, one to use carefully, and most importantly, my world is what I make of it. I was an air pilot calmly navigating through turbulence. And I found a gold mine within. The nuggets unearthed changed my life. I was having a gold rush adventure during a deadly pandemic. I surrendered to the unknown. I heard Wise Jane. As bombs were dropping around me, I found ease and peace through observation. I invested in me and it paid off.

As in YHY (2016), the rewards were immeasurable. I not only survived but thrived—this time without deep fear, pain, and trauma. The fourteen steps I had used for recovery were just as valuable for maintenance. I was navigating emotional roller coasters with more ease. I further healed my headaches, began restoring an uncurable ankle, and joined in partnership with Wise Jane. Miraculous.

I am ready for my next adventure, another treasure hunt perhaps. This time as With Wise Jane (Inner World, 2020–). My YHY arsenal has been repaired and repolished. I am ready to find more gold nuggets. I am eager to continue my life's purpose of being a modern day warrior, rescuing myself to unleash the power and wisdom within. I will share my newest conquests with Wise Jane in my next book, tentatively titled *You Rescue You*. Wise Jane says she's "got my six," so I fully expect it to be a rush of excitement and miraculous. We are on my inner runway, ticket in hand, destination and itinerary unknown. Departure at noon. Stay tuned.

Jane's Glossary

angel track. Nudge from my guardian angels and evidence of their presence. Coincidences are their tracks.

angel wink. Confirmation of an angel track.

(leave your) comfort zones. Do things you fear.

effective medicines. Approaches from Western, Eastern, complementary, alternative, integrative, and holistic traditions from which a unique healing formula is created.

happy healed healer. Someone who has healed, celebrates all of life's experiences, radiates joy, and seeks to inspire others in their journey.

healing partner. Someone who has been where I am and knows where the exit is; someone who has successfully helped others plot a course out of a situation similar to mine; or anyone or anything that helps me. Collectively known as "Jane's Olympians."

Heavenly Team Jane. God and God's squad (including Christ, my guardian angels, and any other divine beings of light), personalized to my needs and in my name. Synonymous with "intuition."

intuition. My inner doctor. An inner knowing that I trust and accept without doubt, question, or explanation. My internal voice that is loud and clear and is not judgmental, negative, or qualified with a "but." When I hear it, I act on it. Synonymous with "Heavenly Team Jane."

Jane's litmus test. If money were no object, would I do this?

Jane's Olympians. My team of carefully selected healing partners.

Jane's Olympics Tryout Checklist. My five-point checklist to screen potential healing partners.

Jane's Treasure Hunt to Wellness. A second-chance game of life, seeking clues (angel tracks) to construct my unique healing formula.

miracle. When something I believe is impossible becomes possible—even if it happens only to me and is not witnessed or understood by anyone else.

modern day warriors. Those who lovingly protect and rescue themselves.

mystical. A spiritual mystery.

spiritual. Relating to the spirit or soul versus to the material or physical.

stairway to joy. My life's journey. Like climbing a stairway, I can go up and down, skip a step, return to a step, and pause on a step or on a landing between steps to rest and reflect. I may even add or refine steps.

unexplained. An event that is beyond ordinary understanding.

unique healing formula. My wellness plan, the mix of healing partners, treatments, and healthy habits from many traditions that is customized to my needs.

What are the odds? A sign that an angel track is present.

woo woo. A supernatural event beyond ordinary experience and scientific explanation, about which I whisper, "woo woo."

You heal you. Take responsibility for your health by doing your part.

YouHealYou™. Organization sponsoring inspirational, self-healing education. Its motto is "inspire, redirect, and heal." Its mission is to inspire others to redirect their thoughts and actions so they can heal.

Acknowledgments

A heartfelt gratitude to Heavenly Team Jane, my intuitive advisory team, for encouraging me to publish a collection of inspirational and miraculous healing stories and then further nudging me to share my own. Much joy and healing has come from this endeavor.

I am beholden to all storytellers in the world who inspire us to keep going and not give up. I am especially indebted to the contributors of *You Heal You*. I would not have done this without your participation. I stand in awe of your courage, accomplishments, and gifts of generosity.

You Heal You would not have taken flight without the love, support, and selfless contribution of Paul Dabrowski. Paul, you are my angel on earth. Thank you for being with me from day one and encouraging me forward. Many thanks to Susie Pappas who unwittingly gave me several useful parables, and to Bobby D for all his healing hugs.

I am blessed to have Lisa Thaler as my editor. Her patience, hard work, attention to detail, creativity, and high level of professionalism made my newest adventure a deeper and more rewarding experience. You are amazing, Lisa. Thank goodness, I followed the angel track leading me to her.

I appreciate and applaud my readers for taking a step towards rescuing yourself. A deep bow to your heavenly team of helpers. Your efforts are what will inspire me to continue walking my stairway to joy.

I thank all of you for being you.

A Conversation with Jane G. Doyle

1. Why do you only talk about your recovery and not give details about your thirty-year trail of terror?

I followed the same discipline in *You Heal You* that I used to heal myself. My survival war cry was Epictetus's philosophy: "It's not what happens to you, but how you react that matters." In other words, "Jane, focus on what you want—feeling well and getting well, instead of on what you don't want—being stuck in the details of my agony." *You Heal You* emphasizes my response to illness, not what made me sick.

2. What made you sick?

My woes started in the early 1980s. In my mid-twenties, I began getting headaches, actually three different kinds of headaches. All day. Every day. It was as if someone turned on a light switch and forgot to turn it off. Three things happened right before my headaches began. I call them my "trifecta of angel tracks" because it sure felt like a heavenly intervention with the odds of their timing, none discovered by tests and each contributing to headaches.

Angel Track #1 Chronic Sinus Infections. While having a cavity filled, a dentist infected a tooth. The root of that tooth went into my sinus and caused frequent sinus infections undetected by x-rays and scans.

Angel Track #2 Body Misalignment. Then, a broken right ankle was incorrectly set, and my bones were fused. For almost thirty years, one leg was shorter than the other, significant by medical standards. The resulting misalignment went unnoticed by my physicians.

Angel Track #3 Whiplash and Head Injury. Finally, while still wearing my walking cast, I was in a head-on collision that totaled both cars. My face hit the steering wheel, and the left side of my head hit the window. Again, my injuries were undetected during screenings.

As the years passed, my symptoms expanded from the initial headaches to chronic fatigue syndrome (CFS) and massive and rapid weight gain; to chest pains, constant neck pain, and continual flu-like symptoms; to ringing in my ears and more. About each of my afflictions, doctor after doctor agreed, "I have no idea why you are experiencing these symptoms."

3. How did a financial professional learn to heal herself?

By the seat of her pants. Understanding medical technology is not my forte. I don't even like the sight of blood. My analytical mind that served me so well in my profession was a detriment during my health struggles. I couldn't analyze my way out no matter how hard I tried. To recover, I had to try something new—rely on my intuition or inner doctor. No prior experience was needed—only the belief that anything is possible, the determination to not give up, and the willingness to work hard.

4. Since most of your healing came from alternative treatments, are you anti-Western medicine?

Actually, I am the opposite. I have great respect for the scientific advances of conventional medicine and a deep sense of gratitude—most recently, for having saved my ninety-year-old mother's life. I am a proponent of all effective treatments from all traditions, such as alternative, complementary, holistic, integrative, and Eastern and Western. If it works, I'm in. My recovery may have been anchored in alternative medicine, but I did not abandon conventional remedies. My unique healing formula leaves a space for Western medicine.

5. What motivated you to write *You Heal You*?

In early 2012, while sitting in the Great Pyramid of Giza, in Egypt, I decided to create a tool I wished I had had while searching for cures of my undiagnosed illnesses. I wanted a book of hope, filled with ideas proven to work for others—something to keep me going when I got stuck and to inspire me when I was fearful, anxious, in pain, and having trouble hearing my inner wisdom.

6. How did you find the seventeen other storytellers? Are their stories true?

Finding stories was the easiest part. The only limitation was if the person was ready to publicly share the experience. Once I set my intent to collect miraculous healing stories, remarkable accounts seemed to randomly come out of the woodwork. They were always around me; I just hadn't noticed them. I was drawn to stories primarily known within their local communities, told by individuals from diverse cultures and backgrounds and representing a range of illnesses. My purpose is to demonstrate that self-healing is universal, and to reach a variety of readers. Each narrative rings true to me; more importantly, does it resonate with you?

7. Why did you adopt three personas—Jane the Apprentice, Jane the Explorer, and Jane the Inspirer—on your healing journey?

These are the names I labeled myself to keep me focused on the task at hand. Each reflects one of my stages of recovery: the apprentice becomes inspired, the explorer seeks cures, and the inspirer heals.

8. Your health crisis was painful, long, frustrating, and expensive, and yet, you harbor no ill will and resentment toward God, any caregiver, or anyone else. How can you be so upbeat after all you've been through?

It is hard to be bitter when you are thankful for an experience. My thirty-year trail of terror helped make me happier and more grateful, and gave me the time of my life writing *You Heal You*. I feel lucky to have received this invitation to change and now, be able to pass it on to others.

9. In chapter 14, you discuss how life is a treasure hunt. How can you believe that with all the suffering and agony in the world?

I realized firsthand that something good can come from something horrific. My experiences changed my perspective. I now view everything that happens to me as a clue in my game of life that ends with a pot of gold.

10. You traveled the world to find your remedies. How will a reader unable to travel become a modern day warrior and self-recover?

I was an armchair traveler during my chronic fatigue syndrome stage. I was inspired by reading angel encounter stories, and then, used the internet to explore the world of wellness. A stay-at-home warrior can be just as effective as a world traveler. Two of my biggest turning points came from me using my computer.

11. If you could talk to your twenty-one-year-old self, what would you say about the next three decades of her life?

I would tell wee Jane that she is about to embark on a life changing adventure. Each upcoming experience is a clue, like playing her favorite game Treasure Hunt, leading to a pot of gold. Earning this reward will require hard work, similar to attaining the grades to attend the University of the South in Sewanee, Tennessee.

When things get challenging, look for ways to be inspired and stay positive. Search for the good in everything. Have faith this is happening for a good reason. You have my word that one day, you will see the reason. When you want things to go easier, pray. It's OK to pause and recharge, but never ever give up.

I would close with: maintain control of your life (and hint, hint, especially your health). You can have a life of joy by doing your part. I promise. Anything is possible with belief, determination, and hard work. So get ready and tighten your seat belt because you're in for the ride of your life.

Made in the USA
Middletown, DE
28 December 2022